Rejoice

Daily Reflections for Easter to Pentecost 2021

Ronald D. Witherup, PSS

LITURGICAL PRESS
Collegeville, Minnesota

www.litpress.org

Nihil Obstat: Rev. Robert Harren, J.C.L., *Censor Deputatus.*

Imprimatur: ✣ Most Rev. Donald J. Kettler, J.C.L., D.D., Bishop of St. Cloud, July 17, 2020.

Cover design by Monica Bokinskie. Cover art courtesy of Getty Images.

ISSN: 2578-7004 (Print)
ISSN: 2578-7012 (Online)

ISBN: 978-0-8146-6517-6   978-0-8146-6541-1 (e-book)

Introduction

Nearly all Christians are familiar with the forty-day penitential season of Lent that leads to Easter. It is a time for prayer, repentance, and almsgiving. In recent times, many have also added the practice of prayerful reading of Scripture (*lectio divina*) as a way to deepen their appreciation of God's Word during this holy season. All of these are good spiritual practices to put our "spiritual house" in order and prepare for the great celebration of the resurrection.

Much less familiar is the fifty-day Easter season that begins on Easter Sunday and leads to the great feast of Pentecost! (The word Pentecost means "fiftieth"; the Christian celebration is rooted in the Jewish harvest festival of the same name, which occurred fifty days after the first sabbath of the feast of Unleavened Bread.) Once Lent is over, many faithful just return to the normal rhythm of life and make no special effort to appreciate what a gift the Easter season is to the church. This is unfortunate because it is the only time in the liturgical year when we hear sequential readings from the Acts of the Apostles—the second volume of Luke's gospel—telling the fascinating story of the birth of the church. It is also a time to recount the multiple stories of the appearances of the risen Lord Jesus, the many encounters with him that emboldened the apostles to preach the gospel message. During this season all the readings, which include excerpts from many of Jesus' discourses in John's gospel describing essential aspects of the Christian faith, lead up to Pentecost, which officially inaugurates the mission of the church to the ends of the earth (Acts 1:8).

This little book is intended to compensate for this lack of attention to a vital liturgical season. Not only will it expose readers to Acts, the New Testament appearance stories, and many parts of the Gospel of John, but also it will address many themes tied to other readings throughout the fifty days that help to give the church its forward-looking, evangelizing thrust. While this book cannot do full justice to the breadth and depth of the Scriptures in this season, it can provide brief, reflective moments each day to deepen your appreciation of God's Word acting in the world and in the life the church *today*.

Alleluia! Christ is risen! He is truly risen! That is the essential message of Easter. Let us celebrate it with joy throughout this holy season.

Reflections

Seeing and Believing

Readings: Acts 10:34a, 37-43; Col 3:1-4 or 1 Cor 5:6b-8; John 20:1-9

Scripture:
Then the other disciple also went in, the one who had arrived at the tomb first, and he saw and believed. (John 20:8)

Reflection: Peter's speech in Acts 10 is a little summary of the essential gospel message: God raised Jesus from the dead and made his disciples witnesses of this truth to proclaim to the ends of the earth. But how difficult it is to believe this message, even though it is at the core of Christian faith!

There is a man, personally unknown to me, who periodically emails me with different versions of the same question: Does the New Testament teach the doctrine of *bodily* resurrection? He is troubled by the concept. (He is not the only one.) It makes no rational sense. After death, we return to dust. How can we resurrect physically? Isn't it more a spiritual resurrection? Or perhaps simply that the spirit of the deceased remains in the memory of loved ones who cherished him or her? Or maybe it only concerns the individual's ideals that remain?

The story of the race to the empty tomb between Peter and the Beloved Disciple on Easter morning illustrates this dilemma. Only the latter immediately perceived the truth;

initially only *he* "saw and believed." Today is not the day to get mired in the details of how Jesus' resurrection took place, or what it means for the resurrection of the dead that he promised his followers. Hundreds of books have tried to explain this mystery, to no full avail. What is clear, though— and the appearance stories we hear throughout the Easter season show this—is that it was the same Jesus of Nazareth who was crucified and was raised from the dead! Transformed, yes, but more than just a memory, more than just a sum of his teachings. For us, as for the first disciples, it comes back to faith—seeing *and* believing.

Meditation: The word that most characterizes the Easter season is *alleluia*. A Hebrew poetic word that means "Yahweh (God) be praised!" it rolls off the tongue almost as a song. Make it a personal mantra throughout the day, quietly reflecting on how God has blessed us through the message of the resurrection.

Prayer: Lord of creation, on this "day of the sun," the first day of the week, I praise and give you thanks for the hope you have sent into the world by vindicating your Son, raising him to new life, and thereby defeating death. Alleluia!

Be Not Afraid

Readings: Acts 2:14, 22-33; Matt 28:8-15

Scripture:
"Do not be afraid. Go tell my brothers to go to Galilee, and there they will see me." (Matt 28:10)

Reflection: Like ripples in a pond into which a stone has been tossed that spread out inevitably to the surrounding shores, so the message of Easter Sunday echoes unceasingly in the first eight days (octave) of the Easter season. Each day is a solemn feast day, filled with sung alleluias, glorias, and joyous songs of the resurrection. "Alleluia, Christ is risen from the dead" resounds over and over and over again. It is easy to forget, however, that there are distinct elements in each of the resurrection appearance stories that we hear.

Today's encounter in Matthew 28 involves the risen Jesus meeting two women from his circle of followers, Mary Magdalene and "the other Mary" (not his mother). His first words to them are, "Do not be afraid." We can assume that the reason for this admonition was the fear and astonishment on their faces. They had witnessed his death on a cross and saw him buried (Matt 27:56, 61). But suddenly there he was in front of them, instructing them to bear the message to Jesus' disciples ("brothers"). Why do we so easily forget that the very first witnesses of the resurrection were *women*? Not the apostles Jesus had chosen! Indeed, ancient tradition calls Mary Magdalene "the apostle to the apostles" because of her unique role as the first to encounter the risen Lord, believe in his resurrection, and announce it to the disciples who carried it forth. Thank God for these faithful women who did not succumb to their fear. Thank God for their witness. In the New Testament, they are shown as the only faithful contingent from the beginning to the end of Jesus' passion, death, and resurrection.

Meditation: Who are the women who have most impacted your own life? Have you done justice to the contributions they made to your well-being, perhaps to your status? Have you ever stereotyped women or denigrated them because of their gender? Pray for women today—and include the fearless Mary Magdalene.

Prayer: Lord, I thank you for my mother who bore me into the world and set me on the right path. Let me never forget her gift to me and the many blessings I have received through the quiet, unassuming role of women who have touched my life. Alleluia!

What Are We to Do?

Readings: Acts 2:36-41; John 20:11-18

Scripture:
"Let the whole house of Israel know for certain that God has made him both Lord and Christ, this Jesus whom you cruci-fied." (Acts 2:36)

Reflection: In October 1989, the San Francisco Bay area suf-fered the traumatic Loma Prieta earthquake that flattened several highways, collapsed a section of the Bay Bridge, caused more than sixty deaths, and damaged many, many structures, including the seminary where I taught. It was a traumatizing experience that induced many sleepless nights as aftershocks continued for months afterwards. One of the reactions I noticed was the frequency with which people asked themselves, "What are we to do?" (We faced the same question as darkness settled that first evening and the extent of destruction to our building was unknown.) The over-whelming job of conceiving how to rebuild one's life in the wake of so much destruction was almost paralyzing. More recent natural disasters have illustrated the same, or even worse, dilemmas.

While today's first reading is not about a trauma, the reac-tion to Peter's dramatic message about Jesus being raised up as "Lord and Christ" nevertheless had a strong effect on the crowd. The text says, "they were cut to the heart," and their reaction was to ask Peter and the other disciples, "What are we to do . . . ?" We cannot know the psychology behind the question, but Peter's response is crystal clear: be baptized and "[s]ave yourselves from this corrupt generation."

Throughout this season, we remember our baptism. It was the seal that launched our Christian identity. Yet it is easy to let it slip into the background and perhaps even fade away. If we really want to know what we should do in light of the gospel message, then re-embracing our faith and putting it into action concretely is the proper response. It means becoming "resurrection people" to all we meet.

Meditation: How conscious are you of your baptism? Have you really "put on Christ," that is, does your life reflect being baptized into Christ Jesus and living in accord with his values? Do you ever worry about what you are to do to put your faith into practice?

Prayer: Praised are you, Lord, for calling me to new birth through water and the Holy Spirit. Enable me to put this divine seal I have received through your grace into action each day of my life. Alleluia!

April 7: Wednesday within the Octave of Easter

Stay with Us

Readings: Acts 3:1-10; Luke 24:13-35

Scripture:
"Stay with us, for it is nearly evening and the day is almost over." (Luke 24:29)

Reflection: It's happened on several occasions. I was having such a good time with family or friends on a festive occasion, and then I noticed the hour. It was time to go. I had a considerable distance to drive and early morning duties at the parish. But then would come the plea: "Can't you stay with us? Just a bit longer?" Well, much as I wanted to, I couldn't. Duty almost always won out.

This experience makes me empathetic to the plea of the two disciples on the way to Emmaus on Easter day. Once they had encountered this fascinating stranger on the road, they naturally wanted him to stay with them. And he did! He immediately "broke bread" with them—in this context clearly eucharistic language—and then their eyes were opened to recognize him. Then they could recall their burning hearts as he had expounded the Word to them and explained the necessity of the Messiah's suffering and death.

"Stay with us" is the cry of the whole church in this season. These words are more than a plea; they are words that reflect a promise. Several gospels reflect this theme, especially in the teaching of the risen Lord (for instance, see Matt 28:20; John 14:3). Even more basic, at each Eucharist the risen Lord Jesus is present in a most intimate way in word and sacrament. He is never apart from us, despite our inability at times to discern his quiet, unassuming presence.

Meditation: Think of the ways in which those who are not physically present in your life at this time are nevertheless still with you. Take the time to name those dearest to you in their absence. Do you feel their presence? Can you experience the Lord Jesus' risen presence as well?

Prayer: Stay with us always, Lord. Do not leave us orphaned, and do not hide your face from us! I trust in your word and in your promises. Alleluia!

All Must Be Fulfilled

Readings: Acts 3:11-26; Luke 24:35-48

Scripture:
"These are my words that I spoke to you while I was still with you, and everything written about me in the law of Moses and in the prophets and psalms must be fulfilled." (Luke 24:44)

Reflection: Skepticism can be a hard reaction to overcome. Once while teaching a group of high school students about the Bible, one of them commented in a loud, sarcastic voice something to the effect that it was just an old book. He saw no real attraction to it. Moreover, he thought it was totally out of date and so could not possibly speak to him. I did not overreact; adolescents sometimes have to "push the envelope," and they need to be led by another path to perceive the value of the past.

But such an attitude is far from the Scriptures themselves. The uniform testimony of the Bible is that God's Word is living and true. It is not a museum-piece or an outdated treatise of ethical teaching. It is a word that spoke to our ancestors in faith and that continues, we believe, to speak to us today in as vibrant a way as ever.

Both readings today emphasize fulfillment of Scripture. For Christians, everything in the Bible is interrelated. The

Old Testament—somewhat simplistically summarized in Luke as the law of Moses, the prophets, and the psalms—prepared for the New, and the New Testament fulfilled what was foretold in the Old. As Peter says, "God has thus brought to fulfillment what he had announced beforehand through the mouth of all the prophets" (Acts 3:18). This is the perspective of faith, of course. Those who block their eyes and ears to the interconnectedness will not necessarily see what we see. Or it may just take more time and careful study. The biblical perspective, however, is clear: all must be fulfilled because God's word is faithful and true.

Meditation: Take a few minutes to reflect on how the Bible can be a "living and true word" for you in your life? What in the Bible "feeds" you, inspires you, or challenges you? How do these words from the Second Vatican Council, based on a teaching of St. Augustine, strike you? "God, the inspirer and author of the books of both Testaments, in his wisdom has so brought it about that the New should be hidden in the Old and that the Old should be made manifest in the New" (*Dei Verbum*, 16).

Prayer: Lord, in your great wisdom, you gave your people your own word as a sure and faithful guide to the truth. May I always appreciate this word for the great gift it is in my life and in the life of the church. Alleluia!

The Rejected Stone

Readings: Acts 4:1-12; John 21:1-14

Scripture:
"He is *the stone rejected by you, the builders, which has become the cornerstone.* There is no salvation through anyone else, nor is there any other name under heaven given to the human race by which we are to be saved." (Acts 4:11-12)

Reflection: The story of Michelangelo's creation of one of his greatest masterpieces, the monumental marble statue of David, is itself remarkable. Begun by an earlier artist who had botched the work and gouged a hole in the marble, the huge slab languished for some twenty-six years, exposed to the elements. Michelangelo (only twenty-six years old) then volunteered to try to redeem the nearly forgotten project for his city of Florence. Genius that he was, Michelangelo perceived that something good could come of this less-than-ideal stone. Although it took incredible artistry and more than two years of delicate carving, he was able to create one of the most stunning images of masculine beauty the world has seen.

The early Christians were accustomed to praying the psalms. Many were Jews and had grown up having memorized psalms for personal and communal prayer. When they prayed Psalm 118, cited in today's first reading, they inevitably thought of Jesus of Nazareth. He was that proverbial stone rejected by the workers as unusable. Ironically, under the hand of the right master builder, it ends up being the "cornerstone" (or keystone), the essential component needed to bring the project to its conclusion! That is why Peter's speech in Acts 4 is so forceful. It asserts that salvation comes to the world through no other means except Jesus Christ. Despite appearances, he alone is the cornerstone, the vehicle of God's salvation. He is the risen Lord of heaven and earth!

Meditation: What surprises you about Jesus' identity as Lord and Savior? Why does God use the unexpected means to accomplish the divine will? How do you understand the assertion that Jesus is the sole means for salvation? How do you think this relates to other religions?

Prayer: Lord Jesus, through your passion and death you were indeed rejected and in a most terrible way. Yet, by the resurrection, you have been vindicated and are the loving Lord and Savior I seek. Accept my humble gratitude through my prayers and commitment to the faith. Alleluia!

Go Forth and Proclaim the Gospel

Readings: Acts 4:13-21; Mark 16:9-15

Scripture:
"Go into the whole world and proclaim the Gospel to every creature." (Mark 16:15)

Reflection: Just the other day, while walking in the rain in a large, multicultural city, I came across a busy intersection where six streets converge. On one corner, in the midst of intense pedestrian traffic, with people going to and fro, a middle-aged, well-dressed man of African descent was screaming at the top of his lungs something about salvation, God, and Jesus. But it was hard to make out the message. So loud was his voice—already raspy from his efforts—and so disjointed his thoughts, I could barely understand what he was trying to say. He was holding a Bible, though, and obviously believed that his message was so important that it had to be announced then and there. Most striking, however, was that not one person in that immense crowd seemed to take any notice of him. They simply skirted round him. Was this a wasted effort? Is this what Jesus meant when he sent out his apostles to proclaim the good news of the kingdom of God to all the world?

We should be careful not to denigrate those who take literally Jesus' command for proclamation. Yet we should also examine ourselves more carefully about the kind of witness we give. Proclamation is a multifaceted word. It can mean orally declaring something, but it can also mean witnessing to a truth in more subtle ways, such as by gestures, by quiet actions not intended to draw attention, and by a life lived in love. Acts clearly shows that the earliest apostles did indeed preach the gospel message in public squares. But more importantly, the early community gained a reputation to be one in fellowship and harmony (Acts 4:32-37).

Meditation: How do you give the most effective witness to being a disciple of Jesus Christ in your life? List three qualities that you believe strengthen your capacity to bear witness to the good news of salvation.

Prayer: Thank you, Lord, for giving me a share in the apostolic mission to announce the good news of salvation to anyone I meet in my daily life. Give me strength to persevere, wisdom to know how best to proclaim your truth, and your mercy for when I fail to live up to this call. Alleluia!

April 11: Second Sunday of Easter
(Sunday of Divine Mercy)

Touch or Do Not Touch?

Readings: Acts 4:32-35; 1 John 5:1-6; John 20:19-31

Scripture:
"Unless I see the mark of the nails in his hands and put my finger into the nailmarks and put my hand into his side, I will not believe." (John 20:25)

Reflection: Was it simply bad timing that occasioned Thomas's absence when the risen Lord appeared to the other ten apostles behind locked doors, or was it that the Lord needed a model for those of us who require a more "tangible" faith? Psychology has pointed out that many people are by nature "sensates"—they need concrete images or objects to help them conceptualize and absorb ideas. They are not intuitive; they resist abstraction. Thomas (or Didymus, the "Twin") apparently was one of this immense group of humanity. The message of the resurrection shared by his brother apostles from an earlier encounter with the risen Lord did not suffice. No, he wanted physical, tactile proof. He certainly got that! Various artists have portrayed vividly this encounter between Doubting Thomas, as we know him, and the risen Jesus. He literally touches the wounds! And then he professes his faith: "My Lord and my God!"

It is not a disgrace to have doubts about faith. The opposite of faith is not doubt, but fear. Thomas needed a more concrete encounter with the risen Lord. Many of us do. Many of us search for easily visible and identifiable signs that Jesus is indeed risen and active in the world we know. Yet note well what Jesus says to Thomas at the end of their encounter: "Blessed are those who have not seen and have believed."

I, like Thomas, would like to touch my risen Lord, yet I know that this privilege belongs only to a few. It is better to be touched by his grace and recognize that what we have received does not come from us but from the free gift given by God.

Meditation: Today is a good time to think of ways that you concretely experience your faith. What images, what saints, what Scripture passages, what prayer rituals, what gestures or prayer positions most express your faith? How has the Lord touched you?

Prayer: Lord Jesus, a humble father concerned for his son once cried out to you, "I do believe, help my unbelief!" (Mark 9:24). It's a prayer with which I can identify. Do not hold my sometimes wavering faith against me. Reach out and touch me, so that I may in turn touch you with a firmer conviction.

Blowin' in the Wind

Readings: Acts 4:23-31; John 3:1-8

Scripture:
"The wind blows where it wills, and you can hear the sound it makes, but you do not know where it comes from or where it goes; so it is with everyone who is born of the Spirit." (John 3:8)

Reflection: In the 1970s, an era that marked me greatly as a "Boomer" in the anti-Vietnam war period, I remember singing a war-protest song titled "Blowin' in the Wind." It was simple and singable yet had a compelling message. How long will it take humanity to learn that war does not work? The refrain provided the answer: "The answer, my friend, is blowin' in the wind." As much as to say, who knows when we will learn the folly of war?

The wind is certainly not easy to get hold of! Yet if you have ever experienced a hurricane or a tornado, as I have, you know its power. Sometimes it roars like a locomotive, sometimes it barely stirs tree branches. While we cannot control it, we can feel it and also harvest its energy, as with wind turbines.

In John's gospel, *wind* (in both the original Greek and Hebrew) can also mean breath, life, and spirit. It is an appropriate image for a reality that we can feel and often hear yet cannot know its origins or its destination. Today's gospel brings us back to this image to remind us once more of our baptism. Touched by God's breath, the Spirit, we have had new life breathed into us, giving us an opportunity to grow in faith. In this case, "blowin' in the wind" is not an expression of doubt or uncertainty, but the opposite. Once touched by this divine wind, we can announce the good news of God's kingdom because we are "born again" (same expression as "born from above"). We are made new by the Spirit of God whom we received by the waters of baptism when the Lord's breath came upon us.

Meditation: Recall experiences in your life you may have had with wind. Which ones were exhilarating? Were any frightening? Why is wind an appropriate image for being born "anew"?

Prayer: Come, Holy Spirit, fill me with your fire and your zeal. Breathe your grace into my innermost being to help me fulfill the promises of my baptism to be born anew every day.

One Heart and Mind

Readings: Acts 4:32-37; John 3:7b-15

Scripture:
The community of believers was of one heart and mind, and no one claimed that any of his possessions was his own, but they had everything in common. (Acts 4:32)

Reflection: Once, when in need of a vacation, I rented a cabin with some friends at a resort that promised gorgeous accommodations, delicious food, a spa, multiple organized activities, and a chance to relax and retool. I should have known that the descriptions, even to the point of the photos on the internet, were too good to be true. The cabin was, to put it mildly, a dump. The furniture and carpets were terribly worn, the bathroom outdated and dirty, and the kitchenette greasy and ill-equipped. The whole place was in serious need of repairs. The spa was "Temporarily Out of Order." The food was, at best, mediocre, though edible. And the group activities ended up being "do it yourself" hikes, games, and the like. Not quite what we had intended, but of course within our price range! I could not help, however, but think of the importance of "truth in advertising." The reality simply did not conform to the ideal.

If one applied similar criteria to the early Christian community, especially as described by Acts, would it fare any better? The opening line of today's first reading, cited above, is almost startling in its promise that all was harmonious with the first Christians. Everyone loved one another; everyone shared their goods in common; all seemed perfect. Too perfect, in fact. One does not have to dig too far into the New Testament to see the community's ideal life tarnished by some less-than-ideal disagreements. Think of the Ananias and Sapphira story (Acts 5:1-11), Paul's confrontation with Peter (Gal 2:11-14), or Paul's lengthy dressing down of the divisions among his beloved Corinthians (1 Cor 1:11-15).

The point on this Easter day, however, is not to prove that all was perfect. Otherwise the New Testament would gloss over the cracks below the surface of the calm. Rather, the celebration points to the *ideal* toward which the church must strain. Attaining the goal is not easy; maintaining the goal before one's eyes is essential.

Meditation: Reflect on the divisions currently experienced in our modern society and in our church. They are clearly multiple. Perhaps the world has never been more divided. Some attribute this situation, to a degree at least, to social media, where people can express themselves with impunity. How can we overcome such divisions? What divisions in your life can you address on a local level?

Prayer: Heavenly Father, you willed that your people would be one, as you are one with your Son, and he with you. Break down the divisions we have created in our world and in our church. Lead us to the deeper unity to which we are called.

April 14: Wednesday of the Second Week of Easter

Not Condemned but Saved

Readings: Acts 5:17-26; John 3:16-21

Scripture:
For God did not send his Son into the world to condemn the world, but that the world might be saved through him. (John 3:17)

Reflection: In her famous work with convicts on death row, Sister Helen Prejean tells multiple stories about the families of murder victims finally coming to the point of recognizing that calls for the death penalty against those who have murdered others is not a path to inner peace. Only working through the complex feelings of hurt, anger, revenge, and restorative justice leads to a place where salvation, not condemnation, rules the world.

In moments of honesty, I confess to harboring a desire for revenge and immediate justice sometimes. Nothing as serious as murder, thank God. But once, on a hazardous curvy highway with a speed limit of fifty miles per hour, some idiot in an expensive sports car was dangerously weaving in and out of traffic at high speed. Drivers were clearly incensed, honking their horns and raising their fists. Lo and behold, a few miles up the road, we passed a state policeman who had miraculously appeared to pull the offender off the road and presumably write him a big ticket. All who drove by beeped their horns in solidarity! Justice in this world had triumphed (for once).

A startling aspect of the Christian message is that "God did not send his Son into the world to condemn" it! Why not? We deserve it, don't we? How is it that people who do bad things often seem to "win," while those who are righteous and striving to do their best seemingly lose? Where is true justice? From a human standpoint, this seems absurd. But it is also the way God is. Expressed in other words, at the beginning of the same gospel reading today, is the famous line found on innumerable evangelical billboards: "God so loved the world that he gave his only-begotten Son . . . " (John 3:16). Good news does not get any better than this.

Meditation: Call to mind those who might have offended you and whom you have found it difficult to forgive. How do you think God views them? Can you see them as also participating in the freely given love and forgiveness achieved in Jesus Christ? As an act of humility, ask God's blessing upon them.

Prayer: I praise and thank you, merciful Lord, for the undeserved gift of your mercy and for not condemning me for my sins, my failings, and my own periodic lack of love.

Like Father, Like Son

Readings: Acts 5:27-33; John 3:31-36

Scripture:
The Father loves the Son and has given everything over to him. (John 3:35)

Reflection: You have likely seen at times, as I have, matching father-son outfits that are worn to make a statement, bring a smile to people's faces, or simply for the fun of it. Once, while shopping in a mall, I came across such a combination that drew a lot of attention. The father was snappily dressed in a color-coordinated yellow shirt, bowtie, vest, slacks, and tan oxford shoes. Walking beside him, dressed in exactly the same outfit, was his son—all of two years old, holding his father's hand and not entirely steady on his feet. Maybe they were on their way to a photo session. Everyone who passed them greeted them with a smile and thumbs-up sign. They were a duo to behold.

One of the chief characteristics of John's gospel, which we hear throughout the Easter season, is the closeness between the Father and the Son. Multiple passages speak of this unified identity. Today the excerpted phrase emphasizes that the Father loves the Son and has given *everything* to him. Elsewhere, Jesus even says that whoever sees him, sees the Father (John 14:9). This goes well beyond appearances. Such assertions reach down to the essentials. Jesus is the face of the Father's glory. That is why celebrating Jesus' resurrection is always related to what his Father has done in and through him. They are one (John 10:30). They act as one. Everything the one does is reflected as a mirror image of the other. This divine duo is incomparable, but it is also intended as a model for us: As they are one, their desire is that we too be one with Jesus Christ and with one another.

Meditation: How close do you feel to Jesus? To his Father? How can you promote a greater closeness to these divine figures who desire to be closer to you than you are to yourself? Spend a few minutes today to ask God to draw closer to you and to shape your life more and more into the mold of his Son.

Prayer: Would that I, heavenly Father, could be as obedient and faithful as your Son! Bestow on me that secure identity of knowing that I am loved and made in your own image.

Fragments

Readings: Acts 5:34-42; John 6:1-15

Scripture:
"Gather the fragments left over, so that nothing will be wasted." (John 6:12)

Reflection: In a recent interview in *Commonweal* magazine, the great American Catholic theologian Father David Tracy spoke of a large project he is working on called "Fragments." He went on to explain how the concept of fragments is so appropriate in theology, but also in life. He views "fragments" as a positive concept that reveals reality as we experience it. There are so many ways in which our lives are never fully integrated into one coherent picture. All too often life is a series of disjointed fragments, which nonetheless tell a unified story. Tracy also views the concept as important for Bible and theology because we can never fully know all the Scriptures or all the tradition; we come into contact with fragments of them.

Today's gospel is John's version of the story of the multiplication of the loaves, the only miracle recorded in all four gospels and in duplicate versions. Here, after the miraculous action of multiplying a boy's five barley loaves and two fish to feed five thousand men, Jesus himself distributes the food. He then commands that the fragments be gathered up so that "nothing will be wasted." Twelve baskets full constitutes a lot of fragments, leftovers enough for a major meal.

Too often, we think of fragments as merely crumbs, hardly enough to bother with. Think of people's fragmented lives, and we could get a similarly skewed picture. Mistakes made along the way, detours taken that led us astray, friendships left to disappear for want of time and care, best intentions never fulfilled.

For God, fragments count for something. They can serve to nourish others. God gathers up our fragments precisely so that nothing goes to waste. It's not just an ecological principle. It's a principle for a life fully valued in each of its parts.

Meditation: Can you identify the "fragments" of your life? Do you see where you may not have fully put into action every opportunity that came your way to make a difference in life, to be a force for the positive, or to show forth your best side? Ask God to help you pull your fragments together to move forward in your life with dignity.

Prayer: Loving Shepherd, you willed that not one of your little sheep, your followers, be lost (John 18:9). You yourself provide the means to ensure that they are protected and held together. Gather up the fragments of my life, and make me see more clearly the identity you have bestowed upon me.

Word *and* Service

Readings: Acts 6:1-7; John 6:16-21

Scripture:
So the Twelve called together the community of the disciples and said, "It is not right for us to neglect the word of God to serve at table." (Acts 6:2)

Reflection: If you were a member of the Hellenist (Greek-speaking believers) community and felt that your widows were being neglected in favor of the Hebrew-speaking ones, you most likely would have jumped on this bandwagon too, in order to convince the twelve apostles to equalize the situation. After all, widows were particularly vulnerable in Jesus' day. They needed male members of the family to care for them, otherwise they would be neglected and marginalized. We do not know exactly all the circumstances surrounding this unusual incident in Acts. What is clear, though, is that the Twelve felt that their primary duty as "apostles" was to proclaim the word of God. Their portrait throughout Acts shows their utter dedication to this ministry. That meant that there was a need for others to step in. Enter the "deacons."

Vatican Council II restored the office of permanent deacon, as distinct from presbyter (priest) or bishop, as a ministry in its own right. While we don't know exactly what the original deacons did beyond serving at table and proclaiming the word, we do know that men *and* women performed this ministry. Paul calls Phoebe (Rom 16:1) a deacon (Greek *diakonos*, a masculine form of the word). They guaranteed proper feeding of the community in bread, while the apostles guaranteed quality of care in the proclamation of the Word. Neither ministry should suffer because of the other. We are the church of word *and* sacrament, proclamation *and* response, Scripture *and* tradition.

The Easter season is a good time to remember this dual action of the Holy Spirit in the life of the church. Just when we are renewing our baptismal vows and recalling the centrality of the Eucharist, the Bread of Life, we are also recalling our need to provide in physical ways through our services for brothers and sisters in need.

Meditation: Consider volunteering for a soup kitchen or similar outreach to the poor, hungry, and homeless in your area, such as the Vincent de Paul Society. If that is not practical, a donation to social services would be most appreciated and would be a way concretely to contribute to the well-being of the community.

Prayer: Lord, your Word is a lamp unto our feet and a light for our path. It helps us not stray from our task of proclaiming good news in word and in deed. Never let me fall into cheapening your Word or sacraments. Rather, let them be front and center in my faith.

The Breaking of the Bread

Readings: Acts 3:13-15, 17-19; 1 John 2:1-5a; Luke 24:35-48

Scripture:
The two disciples recounted what had taken place on the way, and how Jesus was made known to them in the breaking of the bread. (Luke 24:35)

Reflection: One of the most memorable celebrations of the Eucharist I ever presided at happened one Easter Vigil in Alaska. I was sent by the bishop to an outlying island where most of the residents were indigenous peoples. They had not had a priest to celebrate the Triduum (the sacred days of Holy Thursday, Good Friday, and Holy Saturday) for some four years, because of a lack of clergy. When the tiny community learned that there would be a priest present that year, several dutifully showed up to greet me and participate in planning the services. It was quite remarkable. They numbered not more than twenty-five, and they came with ideas. So we planned the various ceremonies, including the baptism of a young infant at the Easter Vigil. Small as we were, and crowded into a nondescript living room that served as a "church," it was nonetheless a powerful experience. As we broke open the Word that night, and as I distributed the consecrated hosts, I felt that I glimpsed something that the two disciples on the road to Emmaus must have experienced.

In those unexpected, sacred moments, feeling the fire in our hearts as the Word was explained and the fire in our bellies as we consumed the bread broken for humanity, we really participated in what Jesus intended: forming a community of faith.

This is not to denigrate other enriching experiences. Cathedrals and churches around the world celebrate magnificent Eucharists. Choirs and well-trained ministers perform their duties with elegance. Large ceremonies can also be uplifting. But even the simplest of Eucharists communicates the same essential truth: we know the Lord in the breaking of the bread. Did not Jesus himself say, "[W]here two or three are gathered together in my name, there am I in the midst of them" (Matt 18:20)?

Meditation: Call to mind one or two experiences of the Eucharist when you really felt close to the Lord. What were the circumstances of those encounters? Whom were you with? What made the experience(s) so special? Say a word of thanks to God.

Prayer: Lord, I thank you for surrounding me with my community of faith and for giving me such worthy sisters and brothers with whom I can celebrate. May our sharing in the sacred mysteries expressed in Word and sacrament bring us closer together.

The Face of an Angel

Readings: Acts 6:8-15; John 6:22-29

Scripture:
Stephen, filled with grace and power, was working great wonders and signs among the people. (Acts 6:8)

Reflection: The feast of St. Stephen, the first Christian martyr, falls on December 26, the day after Christmas. So what's he doing here in the midst of the Easter season?

In recounting the story of the early church, Acts simply records that Stephen, one of the deacons chosen to serve the people of God, was a man "filled with grace and power" who preached with conviction and performed miraculous signs in the name of the Lord. For this, he was persecuted and brought before the Jewish council (the Sanhedrin) with the accusation of blasphemy. Yet when the Sanhedrin gazed on him, today's text says, "his face was like the face of an angel." Presumably, this expression indicates that Stephen confronted his persecutors with sublime tranquility, an inner peace that knows that one is in the right even though the truth will lead to suffering.

There are innumerable stories of persecuted individuals who were falsely accused and yet who peacefully accepted their fate in the face of horrific trials. I think of many heroic stories from the Holocaust, the terrible, unjust killing of millions of innocent people by the Nazis during World War II. St. Maximilian Kolbe comes to mind. This simple Polish Franciscan priest offered his life in exchange for a Jew who was scheduled to be executed but who had a wife and family. Father Kolbe freely offered his life, as did Stephen, knowing full well that he was innocent of any crime yet willingly laying down his life in faith.

Ancient Christian teaching proclaims that "the blood of martyrs is the seed of the church" (Tertullian, d. ca. 240). It began with Stephen, but it did not end with him. It continues today, as thousands of Christians around the world are persecuted simply for being followers of Jesus Christ. In the face of such persecution, we have to admire those who accept their faith with equanimity.

Meditation: Look up the lives of St. Maximilian Kolbe (d. 1941) or of Blessed Franz Jägerstätter (d. 1943), a lesser known Austrian victim of the Holocaust whose story is also inspiring. Versions can be found on the internet and also in film. What do you find inspiring in such stories?

Prayer: Gracious God, giver and sustainer of all life, you have made us human beings "little . . . lower than the angels" (Heb 2:7; see Ps 8:5), yet we know that our actions are not always as angelic as they might be. Strengthen us with the stories of our faithful ancestors so that we might bear authentic witness to the faith.

Forgive, Forgive, Forgive

Readings: Acts 7:51–8:1a; John 6:30-35

Scripture:
"Lord, do not hold this sin against them." (Acts 7:60)

Reflection: Perhaps it is a human tendency, but often the knee-jerk reaction to an offense is to want to seek revenge. Tragically, behind many of the horror stories of mass shootings in the USA is someone's rage at having been slighted, bullied, or offended in some way. Even gang shootings and stabbings often revolve around petty disagreements or perceived turf wars. The only exit in this cycle of violence, as Pope Francis has regularly taught, is to learn the lesson of forgiveness. Mercy is the only medicine that can cure our modern world's ills.

Today's first reading is the continuation of the martyrdom of St. Stephen. Using prophetic language, Stephen points out how "stiff-necked" the Jewish people have been in not living out the Mosaic law that they were given by God to help them discern right from wrong. His words have no effect. His opponents rise up, take him out of the city, and stone him to death. Look carefully at the wording in this text, even in English. Does it remind you of someone else's innocent death (see Luke 23:34, 46)? In fact, some of Stephen's final words reflect the death of his divine Master, Jesus Christ. Like Jesus, rather than cursing his executioners, rather than seeking revenge, he cries out: "Lord, do not hold this sin against them."

The opening words of Pope Francis's promulgation of the "jubilee year of mercy" (2015–16) proclaim: "Jesus Christ is the face of the Father's mercy. These words might well sum up the mystery of the Christian faith. Mercy has become living and visible in Jesus of Nazareth, reaching its culmination in him." To forgive is to apply mercy concretely.

Meditation: Read the first reading slowly to yourself. Then sit in front of a crucifix or a painting of the crucifixion of Jesus for some minutes of meditation. What courage does it take for Jesus, feeling abandoned, in excruciating pain, and being mocked by all around him, to say, "Father, forgive them, they know not what they do" (Luke 23:34)?

Prayer: Merciful and loving Father, grant me a share in the capacity of your Son to forgive and forgive and forgive. Let me never stray far from your own practice to extend mercy and forgiveness even when they are not deserved.

The Promise of Resurrection

Readings: Acts 8:1b-8; John 6:35-40

Scripture:
"For this is the will of my Father, that everyone who sees the Son and believes in him may have eternal life, and I shall raise him on the last day." (John 6:40)

Reflection: Imagine never being hungry again. Or never being thirsty again. Or never having to face suffering again. Or never having to fear death again. What kind of human existence would that be?

Some years ago, an elderly friend of mine suffered a major heart attack. European-born, she was in her mid-80's and had led a remarkable life as a professor at Stanford University. Her heart attack, however, forced her to slow down. In one conversation with me, she admitted that she had always been afraid of death. But after her heart attack, which was truly a near-death experience, she no longer feared death. She felt she had glimpsed "the other side." She confessed that she still feared suffering; she did not like pain. But death itself no longer held any power over her. She believed in the resurrection. She believed she would live forever in God's presence, and that faith sustained her to the end.

One of Christianity's most ridiculed teachings throughout history has been the notion of the resurrection. Various New Testament writings show that it was not an easy concept to swallow (for example, see Acts 17:32). Certainly nothing in Judaism had prepared the Jews for a Messiah to die and rise from the dead, to become the firstborn of many creatures (Rom 8:29). Yet resurrection is at the core of the Christian message. As Paul writes to the Corinthians, "If there is no resurrection of the dead, then neither has Christ been raised. And if Christ has not been raised, then empty [too] is our preaching; empty, too, your faith" (1 Cor 15:13-14).

The entire Easer season is a celebration of Jesus' promise to raise us up on the last day. Our faith is not in vain. The resurrection is not "pie in the sky" or a Hollywood fairy tale. It is a promise of new life, where death will no longer cast its long and fearful shadow over humanity. Most of all, it is a promise of being united with the Creator who first gave us life in this world and now extends it to the next. I believe my friend understood this truth. Once she felt her faith had been confirmed by her experience here below, she was ready to take the next step.

Meditation: How strong is your faith in the resurrection? Have you ever heard people ridicule the idea of the resurrection? How do you respond? Take some time to reflect on family and friends who have died and gone to their eternal rest. Invoke them by name. Do you believe you will one day be reunited with them by means of the resurrection?

Prayer: Lord Jesus, you showed yourself to be the Bread of Life, the Cup of the Salvation, the Resurrection and the Life. I praise you for bringing this hope into the world and for giving us the promise of new life. Comfort me when I doubt this promise and strengthen my resolve to live it.

April 22: Thursday of the Third Week of Easter

Bread of Life

Readings: Acts 8:26-40; John 6:44-51

Scripture:
"I am the bread of life. Your ancestors ate the manna in the desert, but they died; this is the bread that comes down from heaven so that one may eat it and not die." (John 6:48-50)

Reflection: Bread. The very word makes my mouth water. I love *good* bread. I feel very blessed to have been born into a culture where bread is the "staff of life." Being familiar with other cultures, I know well that not everyone lives on bread. For some, rice is the essential ingredient. A meal without rice is unthinkable. For others, a kind of corn meal porridge is the centerpiece for each meal. For me, it's bread. Of course, as I have grown older, I don't eat as much bread as I used to. But if it is freshly baked, and even better right out of the oven, I will dig in every time. It's an original comfort food.

Jesus, too, was born into a culture where bread was important. The Jews normally ate leavened bread, but for certain feasts (especially Passover) unleavened bread was required. This was the bread of suffering, the bread that reminded them that they were once so needy that they had to flee their tyrants without taking the time to let the yeast work its unseen magic in normal bread.

Most dramatic of all is Jesus' action at the Last Supper that we celebrated on Holy Thursday and that we "remember" at each Eucharist. Jesus "took bread" and identified himself with it! "This is my body," he said. And he meant it. To take and eat of this bread is to accept his promise that it is the Bread of Life. As he says in John's gospel, it is not like the miraculous manna that God provided in the desert. That sustained the Jewish people fleeing Pharaoh for a time, but it was not the bread of eternal life. No, this bread is a body offered for the whole world, broken and shared so that all might participate in a new life. Each morsel, each crumb nourishes. It is his "Flesh for the life of the world."

Meditation: What are your favorite breads? Do you know the joy of baking bread? If you have such skill, consider baking some bread for neighbors or family and share it. You might also visit a bakery and soak in the aromas! Good as these are, they are a pale reflection of the Bread of Life. How is Jesus your Bread of Life?

Prayer: Jesus, my Lord and my Savior, I confess that you are the Bread of Life. You provide all that I need. May your Bread not only sustain me but also transform me so that I might carry you to others on my journey of faith.

Chosen Instruments

Readings: Acts 9:1-20; John 6:52-59

Scripture:
"Go, for this man is a chosen instrument of mine to carry my name before Gentiles, kings, and children of Israel, and I will show him that he will have to suffer for my name." (Acts 9:15-16)

Reflection: The dramatic story of the "conversion" of Saul of Tarsus is the focus of the first reading today. True, we celebrate this greatest conversion story in the New Testament on January 25, which also concludes the week of prayer for Christian unity. But it occurs here in the middle of the Easter season because it shows the effect of grace. Even a zealous, hard-headed Pharisee like Saul could have sense knocked into him by an appearance of the risen Lord Jesus.

I place "conversion" in quotation marks because it gives the wrong idea of a change of religion. Paul (the Greek version of his name; Acts 13:9) remained a Jew, albeit one who believed in Jesus as the long-awaited Messiah of Israel. Yet his turnaround was 180 degrees. It was a total transformation. What happened to Saul was nothing short of a prophetic call. As the Lord explains to Ananias, Paul was to be a "chosen instrument," a vehicle to spread the good news that Jesus was indeed the Messiah and the Savior of all humankind. The rest, as the saying goes, is history. Although he never met Jesus of Nazareth in the flesh, he became the foremost among the Apostles. He would be known as "the Apostle" and he would become the greatest letter-writer of the New Testament.

It seems curious that Paul never describes his call with such narrative flair. Instead, he speaks of a "revelation" of Jesus Christ (Gal 1:12), likely meant to describe some mystical experience of the risen Lord that was hard to put into words. Most important, though, is Acts' assertion that Paul was immediately baptized and set off to fulfill the vision of becoming a chosen instrument by proclaiming the gospel message. No hesitance, no questions, no timidity. He never looked back. He went on to become one of the foremost evangelizers in the early church. This is why Paul belongs right in the center of the Easter season.

Meditation: Paul's conversion or prophetic call was dramatic. Most people, however, experience such moments as slow processes, a bit like the dance of life, two steps forward, one step back. Can you identify any such moments in your life? How have you responded?

Prayer: Lord, I feel the urge to say to you, "Here I am, send me." I may lack finesse, I may at times be timid, but I affirm my willingness to be an instrument to spread your good news. Say but the word, and I will go wherever you lead me.

To Whom Should We Go?

Readings: Acts 9:31-42; John 6:60-69

Scripture:
Jesus then said to the Twelve, "Do you also want to leave?"
Simon Peter answered him, "Master, to whom shall we go?"
(John 6:67-68a)

Reflection: The sixth chapter of John's gospel is an extended reflection on the Eucharist. After the miracle of the loaves at the beginning of the chapter, section after section sets forth ways to understand the Eucharist as the Bread of Life. But as Jesus attempts to explain the mystery, more questions emerge. From a logical standpoint, for instance, how can one understand eating someone's body and drinking his blood as anything but some strange cannibalism? This was a charge laid against some early Christians, though they explained in no uncertain terms that that was not the meaning of Jesus' teaching. Jesus' identity as Bread of Life and "living bread" is but a mystery that one must savor at length and reflect on in depth. Alas, many people have neither the patience nor intellectual curiosity to explore this truth.

As the chapter unfolds, various hearers of Jesus' discourse, including some of his own disciples, lose heart and desert. Their "murmurs" against Jesus evolve into actions. They walk away. The text declares that "many of his disciples returned to their former way of life and no longer walked with him."

No wonder Jesus' question to the Twelve arises. If he's losing disciples at each step along the way, it would not be unreasonable to suspect the Twelve, too, will succumb. They could become tired, too. They could lose heart because clarity over the mystery of the living bread is not forthcoming. Then comes the poignancy of Simon Peter's response: "Master, to whom shall we go?" In the end, Simon Peter's faith wins out, for he admits that only Jesus has "the words of eternal life."

The mysteries of faith, such as the Eucharist, can baffle and frustrate us. The temptation to let it all drop can be great. In such moments, think of Simon Peter's response. It is still the best.

Meditation: Have you ever been tempted to give up on a very difficult task or a conundrum? Perhaps it concerned a relationship gone sour, or a complex mathematical problem, or a task at work that seemed too complicated. What gets people through these tough situations? For an even more essential issue, namely our faith, what keeps you going?

Prayer: When I am tired and impatient, Lord, strengthen my resolve not to follow the easier path of others who give up and go their own way. Don't abandon me when I am tempted to abandon you. I promise my best to abide.

April 25: Fourth Sunday of Easter

A Really Good Shepherd

Readings: Acts 4:8-12; 1 John 3:1-2; John 10:11-18

Scripture:
"I am the good shepherd, and I know mine and mine know me, just as the Father knows me and I know the Father." (John 10:14-15a)

Reflection: The story of the American missionary and martyr, Blessed Stanley Rother (d. 1981), is as simple as it is profound. When asked why he did not flee Guatemala when his life was being threatened for his work among the poor, he quipped, "The shepherd cannot run at the first sign of danger." He stayed. He was martyred. He was a modern incarnation of the Good Shepherd.

John 10 is the most poetic and lengthy reflection on the image of the Good Shepherd. The image, which clearly comes from a rural agricultural setting common to Jesus' native Galilee, still resonates even in our modern, industrial world. It's all about fidelity. It also concerns proximity, the closeness between a shepherd and his sheep. Jesus insists that his laying down his life for the sheep is not a fluke, nor is it a miscarriage of justice. He lays down his life freely, but with all confidence, he knows that he can take it up again because his Father will not abandon him.

Jesus' teaching is not naïve. He knows that there are shepherds who are not particularly good. Some act like "hired hands." The minute they perceive some danger, they will hightail it out of town. Moreover, unlike true shepherds, hired hands don't view the sheep as their own. They're merely a job, a source of income. He has no real interest in *them*, which is why such shepherds disappear at the first sign of trouble.

This beautiful Johannine teaching has an Old Testament background as well. Originally, Israel relied only on God as their shepherd (= king). But when they pleaded with God to give them an earthly shepherd and they failed miserably at shepherding the people, God promised to shepherd them once more himself (Ezek 34:1-31). Jesus is that true Shepherd. And because he and the Father are one, they are in this together. The shepherd has returned to the flock!

Meditation: Go to your Bible and open Ezekiel 34. Take the time to read the chapter, keeping in mind today's gospel passage, which proposes Jesus as the fulfillment of God's promise to shepherd his own people.

Prayer: Jesus, my dear Shepherd, I praise and thank you for protecting me, for protecting your whole flock, the church. We would be lost without you. Thank you for your faithfulness.

The Doorway

Readings: Acts 11:1-18; John 10:1-10

Scripture:
"I am the gate. Whoever enters through me will be saved, and will come in and go out and find pasture." (John 10:9)

Reflection: As a youth I loved the music of Simon and Garfunkel. I was also an amateur musician and enjoyed playing much of their music. One song had a South American flavor. It was intriguing and haunting. It was titled "El Cóndor Pasa (If I Could)." The opening lines were: "I'd rather be a sparrow than a snail, / Yes, I would, if I could . . ." I wonder if we could not add a line, something like, "I'd rather be a gate than a fence / Yes, I would, if I could . . ."

Whatever the intention of the original song, its sentiment is about choosing the better of two options, if one could. Wouldn't it be better to be a gate than a fence? Wouldn't you rather be an instrument for communication and concourse than a means of blocking such relationship?

Today's gospel is a continuation of the shepherd image. It employs the related figure of the gate and the gatekeeper. Unlike fences, gates allow creatures to enter or leave. They function like doorways. The gatekeeper is charged to see that only proper creatures enter or leave, so no thieves or robbers can come in and steal what is not theirs. Jesus asserts that he is the gate *and* the gatekeeper. He knows all his sheep and can let them come and go as he calls them by name.

We Christians often use the image of a "doorway" to speak of death. In fact, St. Paul insists that by baptism we entered into the tomb with Christ, in order that we might come out on the other end with Christ in the resurrection (Rom 6:4). So, baptism is a kind of doorway, too. Christ opened it for us. He invites us through it.

Meditation: In what ways is your life more like a gate or a door than a fence or a wall? Reflect on ways you have benefitted from Jesus' message that he functions as a gate so that he can protect his flock.

Prayer: Loving Shepherd and kindly gatekeeper, lead me onward through your gate and under your protection, that I might receive the fullness of life you promised.

April 27: Tuesday of the Fourth Week of Easter

Christian, Wherefore Art Thou?

Readings: Acts 11:19-26; John 10:22-30

Scripture:
It was in Antioch that the disciples were first called Christians. (Acts 11:26)

Reflection: St. Augustine is one of the church's greatest and most influential theologians of all time. He was a convert to Christianity, thanks to his mother's incessant prayers and God's grace. Among the many insights of his writings, he made this comment when he was surprisingly elected bishop in Hippo (North Africa): "For you I am a bishop, with you, in fact, I am a Christian. The former title speaks of a task undertaken, the latter of grace; the former betokens danger, the latter salvation." Augustine's words evoke the heart of the matter about Christian identity. It is a graced call and one that brings with it salvation, not privilege. It means following the one whose name stands above all others, Jesus, the Christ.

According to Acts, Antioch (in Syria) was the place where disciples became known as Christians. Was this a self-designation or an external label? This is not clear. What is clear is that the name likely began in Antioch because already the presence of non-Jews (= Gentiles) among the believers was hinting at what would become a separation from Judaism. There would come a parting of the ways in which the name *Christian* would clearly indicate a separate type of existence. Over time, the label would become a kind of badge of courage. Just as Christ himself suffered, so did his followers. Christians thus were those who accepted the fate of their master with equanimity and with honor.

In the early church, in times of persecution, those arrested were interrogated about their identity. Many stories of the martyrs list the simple response that most would give to the authorities: *Ego Christianus sum* ("I am a Christian"). From a faith perspective, identity does not get any simpler. Being a follower of Christ is the only thing that counts.

Meditation: Are you proud of your Christian identity? What does it really mean to call yourself a Christian? Are you worthy of the label? As one author put it, if you were being judged as a Christian, would there be enough evidence to convict you?

Prayer: Lord, by baptism, you bestowed on me the dignity of becoming a follower of your Son. Strengthen my resolve to put this identity into action, even if it means that I should suffer for the sake of your name.

April 28: Wednesday of the Fourth Week of Easter

Looking Beyond

Readings: Acts 12:24–13:5a; John 12:44-50

Scripture:
"Whoever sees me sees the one who sent me." (John 12:45)

Reflection: Is seeing always believing? Apparently not. Once I was visiting the Grand Canyon with some friends. We had just arrived and were standing at the edge of the south rim of the canyon, awestruck at the grandeur stretching out for miles before us. Along came a family of visitors from France. They were standing near us so that it was easy to overhear their conversation. They presumed, I imagine, that no one nearby could understand French. But I did. And to my astonishment, one of the elderly visitors shrugged and, before turning away, said to those around him, "Eh, it's just a big hole in the ground."

Just a big hole? I could scarcely imagine someone not being impressed by this awesome work of creation. But there it was. He could not *see* what virtually everyone else saw. He could not transcend the mundane composition of the canyon to see its breathtaking beauty.

When Jesus of Nazareth walked amidst his disciples and the crowds, a bit of the same phenomenon occurred. Some could look beyond this simple peasant from Galilee and see the image of the Father. But not everyone could. Jesus asserts in today's gospel that anyone who sees him sees "the one who sent me." But this still requires the eyes of faith. Even his disciples seemingly missed the point on occasion.

John Ruskin, the great nineteenth-century art critic and philosopher, once wrote, "The greatest thing a human soul ever does in this world is to *see* something, and tell what it saw in a plain way. Hundreds of people can talk for one who can think, but thousands can think for one who can see. To see clearly is poetry, prophecy, and religion—all in one." Ruskin had the eyes of an artist, a poet, and a philosopher. He could see beyond and knew the value of this deeper vision. I sometimes wonder what I would have seen if I had lived in the time of Jesus. Would I have perceived the work of his Father, the Creator of the universe? Or would I have been blind to the truth before me?

Meditation: I recommend an exercise in imagination. Take some moments to place yourself in first-century Palestine, in Jerusalem, in the company of Jesus and his apostles. What do you see? How does Jesus come across to you? What do you find attractive in him? Is there anything disturbing? How would *you* have responded to his teachings?

Prayer: Grant me true vision, heavenly Father, so that I may learn to look beyond what is right in front of me and see the work of your hands, especially through your Son Jesus Christ.

Masters and Servants

Readings: Acts 13:13-25; John 13:16-20

Scripture:
"But so that the Scripture might be fulfilled . . . " (John 13:18)

Reflection: Monasteries are wonderful places to visit, especially to experience silence and to be renewed spiritually. I have visited many monasteries, especially Benedictine ones, and have noticed something fairly common. Sometimes, upon arriving and being received by the guest master, and then joining the entire community for prayer or a meal, it is not always easy to determine right away which monk is the abbot. That is often by design. The abbot, although the spiritual father of the community, is also a member of it and sometimes slips indiscernibly into their midst to be at their service. Of course, on certain occasions the abbot presides and is visibly the head of the community. Many times, however, he is simply in the community.

Today's gospel comes just after Jesus has washed the feet of his disciples. We celebrated this novel event on Holy Thursday evening at "the supper of the Lord." Jesus' action—doing the most menial task of the lowest servant—is specifically intended as a *model* for his disciples. No slave is greater than his master, says Jesus, but the true "master" is the one who serves all the others! There is a merger, of sorts, of the roles. Master does not mean lording it over others and being a servant does not mean being only at a master's beck and call. What Jesus did by taking on the form of a slave (see Phil 2:7) is for the fulfillment of Scripture. In fact, the entire liturgical year is a celebration of how the Scriptures, as the Word of God, have been fulfilled in the story of Jesus and the founding of the church. Through word and deed, Jesus taught the truth by example. As he did, so we his followers are to do. We are not greater than the Master, but we are to put into practice what he himself lived.

Meditation: What concrete gesture can you do today to assist others, whether in your family, among your friends, at work, or in the community? Perhaps volunteer for some social service, perhaps visit someone in a nursing home, perhaps shine someone's shoes, perhaps clean someone's room or apartment.

Prayer: Lord Jesus, you taught us by example and not only by word, and for that I am grateful. Help me to become a true servant to others and not to seek positions of honor.

Not Abandoned Orphans

Readings: Acts 13:26-33; John 14:1-6

Scripture:
"And if I go and prepare a place for you, I will come back again and take you to myself, so that where I am you may also be." (John 14:3)

Reflection: Watching the news one evening brought tears to my eyes. (Actually, that probably happens more often than not!) A report about the seemingly endless conflict in Syria and the Middle East featured the horrible impact on children who had been left orphaned by the war. One case was particularly troubling. A beautiful little girl of about five or six would not say a word. Nor would she let go of a Red Cross worker who had been working with her to try to heal some of the trauma she had experienced. Her family had been killed by bombs. She was totally orphaned. She would not smile; she would not speak. Neither would she cry. The terror in her eyes spoke volumes.

This child's case, sadly, is not the only horror tale. Children all too often are the terrible victims of war and violence. The trauma often ruins them for life. Orphaned, they feel unloved, forgotten, and without a secure identity.

Surely, the early disciples did not view Jesus' words about returning to his Father with the same amount of emotion. Yet a theme in the Fourth Gospel is that Jesus had come from the Father and had to return to the Father. What would happen to the disciples, then? The words of today's gospel respond to this question. Jesus invites them to remain untroubled and reassures them, "In my Father's house there are many dwelling places." He also provides the rationale. He departs from them in order to prepare "a place" for them. He will, in fact, return in order to bring them along. So he is not leaving them orphaned but going to prepare a welcome for them.

There is even more depth to this teaching than we can describe here. The essential theme is clear, however. Jesus does not abandon his disciples. The vocabulary of John's gospel is reassuring. Jesus "dwells" with them, he "remains" with them, he "abides" with them, and he invites them into this indwelling (John 14:10, 17, 25; 15:1-10, the Greek word *menein*).

Meditation: Why do you think Jesus wants us to dwell with him? What can we offer heaven? Have you ever felt abandoned? What did you do to counter this feeling? Thank the Lord in prayer for knowing that you will never be abandoned by God.

Prayer: Abide with me, dear Lord, as I wish to abide with you. Please prepare my place in your kingdom where I hope to join you in the presence of all the saints whom you have welcomed home.

May 1: Saturday of the Fourth Week of Easter
(Saint Joseph the Worker)

From the Shadows

Readings: Acts 13:44-52; John 14:7-14, or, for the Memorial, Gen 1:26–2:3 or Col 3:14-15, 17, 23-24; Matt 13:54-58

Scripture:
Is he not the carpenter's son? (Matt 13:55a)

Reflection: This optional memorial of the foster father of Jesus of Nazareth dates from the Middle Ages. Only in modern times, under Pope Pius XII in 1956, did it become oriented to dignifying work from a Christian perspective. It was established, in part, to counter the growth of the socialist, secular celebrations of May Day.

For many people, work is a four-letter word. Some see work as almost a nasty concept. It means having to labor. Many people look forward to retirement so that they never have to "work" again. The book of Genesis addresses the issue. God's act of creation is said to be "work." And on the seventh day (hence the sabbath) God "rested . . . from all the work he had undertaken" (Gen 2:2). If God can work, why shouldn't we? We are, after all, made in God's image.

For Catholics, Joseph has become an icon of the dignity of work, although on other feast days in the liturgical year his role as foster father takes precedence. In Scripture, Joseph is the great silent figure. He utters not a word, although in

Matthew he is the recipient of some "dreams" (like his Old Testament namesake) that help save Jesus and his mother from King Herod. Today's gospel simply indicates in a back-handed way that Jesus was his "son"—the son of a carpenter, the only place where Joseph's trade is mentioned.

The question for some who admire Joseph as the quiet masculine type is how to bring him out of the shadows. Pope Francis did that somewhat when he ordered that Joseph's name was to be inserted into the other Eucharistic prayers of the Mass, as had already been the case for half a century in Eucharistic Prayer I (the Roman Canon). So now at each Mass, Joseph is named as the spouse of the Virgin Mary.

Meditation: Do you know anyone named Joseph? Wish them a blessed feast day today and say a prayer for them and their loved ones. Do you know anyone who hates their work? Initiate a conversation with them about the pros and cons of work and how to make the most of it.

Prayer: Lord, Creator of the universe, when I grow weary of all the work I must do, remind me of how to slow down. Remind me also of the value that an honest day's work can bring to my life and my family.

Staying Connected

Readings: Acts 9:26-31; 1 John 3:18-24; John 15:1-8

Scripture:
"I am the vine, you are the branches." (John 15:5)

Reflection: Many of the down-to-earth images used in the gospels come from an agricultural setting. The vine mentioned in today's gospel is likely intended to be a grape vine. Grapes were obviously important in first-century Palestine (and today!), as a source of both fruit and wine. Once I was helping a woman in her garden, which unfortunately was overgrown, owing to a lack of consistent attention. In one corner, the presence of weeds was clearly evident. She explained to me that she had a particular problem with this one area because of the presence of a tenacious, invasive species of vine. Once it got hold of other plants, even trees, it seemed impossible to cut back. Eventually it could choke off the native plants. She had tried again and again, cutting off many branches. Yet they would grow back. She had to learn from another gardener that the only way to destroy the plant was to cut it off at the base and rip out the roots; cutting the branches was not sufficient.

In this Easter season we celebrate the fact that our "true vine," Jesus Christ, could never be defeated. It was he who defeated death by the power of the resurrection. But for his followers, unless we remain tied to him, it is easy for us to be cut off. Only by remaining in him can we endure. As Jesus explains, "Whoever remains in me and I in him will bear much fruit, because without me you can do nothing."

The power to live out our baptismal promises as followers of Jesus is not our own. It comes only from him, the source of all life and goodness. That is why it is so important to remain tied to him. We remain in him just as he remains in us. Together, vine and branches, we can flourish and produce much fruit.

Meditation: How closely connected do you feel to the risen Lord Jesus? Have you ever experienced going astray from him? Today might be a good Sunday to sip a glass of wine or enjoy a handful of grapes while reflecting on the lovely image of the vine and branches. Thank God for the fruit of the vine!

Prayer: Lord, giver and sustainer of all life, I desire always to remain tied to you and to take my nourishment from you. Do not let me be cut off from your mercy or stray from the lifeline that you provide.

Two by Two

Readings: 1 Cor 15:1-8; John 14:6-14

Scripture:
"Master, show us the Father and that will be enough for us."
(John 14:8)

Reflection: A remarkable aspect of the gospel message is the
presence of two sets of *brothers* in Jesus' inner circle. Remember
Andrew and Simon (John 1:40-42)? How about James
and John the sons of Zebedee (Mark 1:19-20)? More broadly,
when Jesus sent out his disciples for their missionary activity,
they went "two by two," not singly (Mark 6:7; see Luke 10:1).
Today's feast also calls to mind this same principle. Though
Philip and James were not brothers, they are remembered
together for their apostolic mission. Philip is the one who
says the words cited above, which brings Jesus' astonished
response that Philip and the others have not yet understood
that to see *him* is to see the Father.

Our baptismal call is certainly individual. Yet it is also a
call to become part of a new family. Interestingly, Jesus seemingly
set membership in this new family of faith above that
of blood kinship (see Mark 3:31-35), but he began by calling
brothers to him to form the foundation of the Twelve, the
symbolic reconstitution of the tribes of Israel. We do not enter
the apostolic circle alone. We enter together, and we are sent

out on mission together. Why? Are not two heads better than one? Two sets of eyes better than one? Two individuals more supportive, the one for the other?

A further comment may be helpful here. Although Jesus called men to be members of the Twelve, women held a vital place in the same community. They certainly followed Jesus as a group throughout his ministry (see Luke 8:2; 23:49, 55), although always in the background. Even more telling is that, unlike the Twelve, who fled on the night Jesus was betrayed (Mark 14:50), the women were the faithful ones. They are the ones watching from a distance on Calvary (Matt 27:55), bold enough to visit the tomb on Easter Sunday morning (Matt 28:1), and the very first to receive the message of the resurrection (Mark 16:1). As time went on, they became important figures in ministry, such as companions of Paul, many of whom were women (Rom 16:1-16).

Meditation: Who are your best companions in the faith? Your spouse? Your family? Certain faithful friends? Certain parishioners with whom you identify or work? Call to mind any of these colleagues, and say a prayer for them. We are in this community together.

Prayer: I rejoice, Lord, in those you have gathered around me to urge me on and to collaborate with my efforts in the faith. Bless my colleagues and keep them close so that we might support one another.

What Are Friends For?

Readings: Acts 14:19-28; John 14:27-31a

Scripture:
Your friends make known, O Lord, the glorious splendor of your kingdom. (Responsorial Psalm)

Reflection: Today's readings are a good follow-up to yesterday's theme. After Paul suffers serious persecution in Lystra, he is joined by others who "strengthened the spirits of the disciples" and gave them the courage to continue with their missionary outreach. The psalm response expresses the sentiment that God's friends are the ones who make known the "glorious splendor" of the kingdom. True friends are vital in life. Apart from family, they are the ones who most sustain us when times are difficult or when doubts assail us.

Jesus himself recognizes the power of friendship. A theme in John's gospel, in fact, expresses the transformation Jesus initiates when he says he no longer considers his disciples slaves (or servants) but friends (John 15:15). He reinforces this close connection by also saying that a true friend is one who lays down his life for his friends (John 15:13). That is how close friends are to be and how much they are to support one another.

What are friends for? A proverb whose authorship is now unknown speaks of friendship in these words:

Don't walk behind me; I may not lead.
Don't walk in front of me; I may not follow.
Just walk beside me and be my friend.

Friends mostly accompany us. They help us remain true to our identity. They can keep us on the straight and narrow path without being judgmental. And they accept our faults for what they are—imperfections on a journey.

Jesus clearly valued friendship. He spent time with his friends, he taught them, he ate and drank with them. Even when they abandoned him, he did not judge them but felt only sorrow at their weakness. In this Easter season, we strive to restore the power of that friendship the gospel proclaims.

Meditation: Name the friends who mean the most to you. How well do you treat them? How deep do you believe your friendship to be? Say a prayer for each one of your friends and resolve to spend a little more quality time with them.

Prayer: Lord, my God, you have deigned to offer me your friendship, and you have graciously invited me into the circle of your friends. May my voice join theirs to proclaim the glories of your kingdom forever!

Pruned and Ready to Bloom

Readings: Acts 15:1-6; John 15:1-8

Scripture:
"You are already pruned because of the word that I spoke to you." (John 15:3)

Reflection: I know several people who have fruit trees in their backyards. They live in a climate that supports such trees as figs, oranges, lemons, persimmons, avocados, and the like. One of these had the habit of neglecting his trees. Somehow, he never got around to pruning them at the right time. After a few years, he got little fruit. He would water and fertilize them, but he never realized that the key was to prune them. Only by seriously cutting back parts of the trees that drain the energy can they produce an abundance of good fruit. Another of my friends did just that, and the results were exactly what she had hoped.

In Paris, where I lived for many years, the practice of the city was to go through the many beautiful gardens and tree-lined boulevards and severely prune them in winter. In fact, I thought the pruning so severe that I was sure the trees would never bounce back. They were almost devoid of branches. How could they rebound? Yet year after year they did come back. Not only with thick branches and full leaves, but artistically shaped just the way they were desired. It seems severe pruning can be even more productive (though I won't accept responsibility if it doesn't work in your garden!).

Pruning, of course, is an agricultural metaphor Jesus uses of his disciples in today's gospel. It is not meant literally but figuratively. Yet the effect is supposed to be the same. Pruning is good for the soul. It allows the deeper nourishment to come to the surface and to shape our faith more effectively.

Meditation: What do you think it means to be "pruned because of the word"? Does this mean that the word cuts to the quick, or makes you confront yourself?

Prayer: Dear Lord, I acknowledge my need to be pruned in my life so that I might produce a better fruit by my Christian lifestyle. Prune me tenderly, but shape me to your own desire!

Signs and Wonders

Readings: Acts 15:7-21; John 15:9-11

Scripture:
The whole assembly fell silent, and they listened while Paul and Barnabas described the signs and wonders God had worked among the Gentiles through them. (Acts 15:12)

Reflection: We were gathered around a campfire listening to a friend tell the tale of his hiking alone in the woods in the Canadian Rockies (not a recommended method for hiking, by the way). He described an encounter with a bear, which fortunately fled in the other direction. Then he spoke of taking a short sit-down break to eat a snack. He was positioned on a ledge across a narrow valley. While seated there entirely alone, the mountain on the other side of the valley suddenly collapsed. Avalanche! It was so powerful he could actually feel the air move as the force of the fall rushed across the narrow valley. And he alone witnessed it! The tale was well told. You could hear a pin drop—except that we were in a forest ourselves!

The Acts of the Apostles has numerous stories to tell of the "signs and wonders" God accomplished as the apostles made their way on their missionary journeys. It is easy to imagine assemblies falling silent as the apostles later told their tales. The conversion of the Gentiles, which is the context of today's first reading, was such a remarkable and unexpected development that it was bound to stun audiences hearing about it. In his letters, Paul is clear that all this happened by the grace of God. In Acts, it is clear that the Holy Spirit is the engine driving this growth. Either way, it is God's action that is being celebrated. The Christ event had happened for all humanity and not simply for the chosen people, the Jews. As Acts unfolds, it is clear that God is allowing boundaries and walls to fall so that all may enter and share the new life initiated by the cross and resurrection of Jesus.

Meditation: What signs and wonders do you believe you have witnessed in your life? These may not qualify technically as miracles but perhaps remarkable turnarounds or unexpected developments. Give thanks to God for witnessing such events.

Prayer: Praised are you, Lord God of all creation, for you continue to work wonders in this world despite all its limits. Never withhold your grace from us, as we place all our hope in you.

Love One Another

Readings: Acts 15:22-31; John 15:12-17

Scripture:
"This is my commandment: love one another as I love you."
(John 15:12)

Reflection: Every Christian knows that the core of Jesus' teaching revolves around love. He summarized the whole law and the prophets as two intertwined commandments, love of God and love of neighbor (already foreseen in the Old Testament; see Deut 6:5 and Lev 19:18). In John's gospel, he repeats multiple times the one and only new commandment: love one another as I love you.

I fear however, that many of us have an inherent stumbling block regarding this commandment. As clear and simple as it is, it is not easy to put into practice. I am haunted by a *Peanuts* cartoon from Charles Schulz (d. 2000) in which the character Linus, the theologian of the gang, admits, "I love [hu]mankind . . . It's *people* I can't stand!"

In theory, love seems an easy principle to proclaim. What could be so difficult? Until you start thinking of all the annoying ways in which many individuals you know grate on you. They have this or that fault. They dress this or that odd way. They are prejudiced or intolerant or greedy or dishonest or snooty or have bad breath or whatever. Living with one another, warts and all, is not easy. But then Jesus never promised that love was easy. Acts itself shows that the early church could be discordant. The Johannine writings of the New Testament show the same thing. Apparently, interpretation of the Gospel of John itself became a battleground, even over the concept of love and how it should be lived out (see the three letters of John).

Yet none of this negates or even minimizes Jesus' love commandment. Paul, too, made it a centerpiece of his ethical teachings. He tells the Galatians, who are engaged in infighting: "[T]he whole law is fulfilled in one statement, namely, 'You shall love your neighbor as yourself'" (Gal 5:14).

Meditation: Examine your own attitudes and behavior honestly. Where do you fall short of living out the love commandment? Can you see where it might be possible to modify your stance in light of Jesus' teaching? A place to begin is to say a brief prayer for those who annoy you.

Prayer: Lord, I want to love as you loved. Be patient with me as I move forward. May the joy and hope of this Easter season encourage me along the path of love.

Truth *and* Consequences

Readings: Acts 16:1-10; John 15:18-21

Scripture:
"If the world hates you, realize that it hated me first." (John 15:18)

Reflection: Most people are familiar with the expression "truth or consequences." Tell the truth or face the consequences. The condition often occurs in the context of people caught in a web of lies. If they don't come clean, they could face serious consequences, legal or otherwise.

For today's liturgical celebration, I suggest a more appropriate adage: truth *and* consequences. The little conjunction "and" makes all the difference. Jesus' teaching in today's gospel provides the hint of why this saying is so important in this Easter season. He warns his disciples with clarity: "If the world hates you, realize that it hated me first." A few lines later he adds: "If they persecuted me, they will also persecute you." There is not a lot of fudging here. The fact that the world did "hate" Jesus, even to the point of seeking his death, means his followers inevitably are going to be hated too. Though today's reading from Acts describes in glowing terms the spread of the faith through the ministry of Paul and colleagues, even to the European continent, it is only a prelude of what is to come. Eventually, opposition will mount and persecution will set in. Arrests will be made, imprisonment will arrive, and all kinds of persecution. All this, because what they did to the Master, they will do to the disciples (see also Matt 10:16-18).

Throughout the Easter season we have heard of some witnesses to this persecution. We have seen Christians pay the price. We know it still goes on today. In the Middle East and Africa, for instance, the unsettled nature of society and the ongoing conflicts and wars are killing Christians and/or driving them away. All for speaking and living the truth of the gospel of Jesus Christ. It really is truth *and* consequences.

Meditation: Gather some family or friends together to talk briefly about the suffering church of our times. Perhaps reread the stories of a few martyrs and speak of your reactions. How might you witness to the faith without having to undergo such severe trial?

Prayer: Loving God, as I sit in my rather comfortable life, filled with many blessings you have given me, do not let me become complacent in my faith. Embolden me to be a witness to your truth in whatever little ways possible.

Divine Impartiality

Readings: Acts 10:25-26, 34-35, 44-48; 1 John 4:7-10; John 15:9-17

Scripture:
"In truth, I see that God shows no partiality. Rather, in every nation whoever fears him and acts uprightly is acceptable to him." (Acts 10:34-35)

Reflection: The beloved American poet Robert Frost (d. 1963) wrote a magnificent poem that I read periodically, titled "Mending Wall." It recounts the tale of two New England neighbors whose properties abut one another where a wall has fallen into disrepair. The first line begins with the observation: "Something there is that doesn't love a wall." As the story continues, however, the voice of the other neighbor is quite insistent to repeat the adage "Good fences make good neighbors." He is not happy that the wall is crumbling and that the two properties will blur somehow.

Suspend for a moment the logic that boundaries, especially in a modern, litigious society, can be good markers. Fences do serve a purpose; they make boundaries and rights and obligations clear. But there is something much deeper afoot in the Frost poem. It concerns boundaries we set up around ourselves that are really *false* walls, intended to keep people out rather than welcome them in.

The early Christians—and Acts does not deny this—struggled with just how wide God's mercy extended. How could it include the Gentiles, those pagans who were not part of the covenant? It was a debate hotly contested at the council of Jerusalem narrated in Acts 15 (see Paul's version of it in Galatians 2). Ultimately, even Peter and James, leaders in the Jewish mother church in Jerusalem, came to see that God shows no partiality. Anyone can belong to this new faith. The only criterion was accepting Jesus Christ and living an upright life.

Meditation: Find a copy of Frost's poem "Mending Wall," easily available on the internet or in collections of American poetry. Sit with it and mull it over. What does it say to you in the context of the Christian teaching that God shows no partiality?

Prayer: Loving Father, how broad and deep and wide is your mercy that draws all to yourself! Never let me become stingy in sharing what you have so freely given me—your love, your mercy, your forgiveness.

An Advocate of Truth

Readings: Acts 16:11-15; John 15:26–16:4a

Scripture:
"When the Advocate comes whom I will send you from the Father, the Spirit of truth who proceeds from the Father, he will testify to me." (John 15:26)

Reflection: You have probably seen television ads, as I have, for law firms. I find them annoying. Many of them come across as "ambulance chasers." They claim that for no money down and no payment unless you win the case, they will be your advocate. They will stand by you to prove that you were wronged. Perhaps it was an injury at work or an automobile accident or a botched surgery. They will defend you or adjudicate your injury. None of this necessarily seems to have any bearing on the truth of the matter. Some people may well be wronged and deserve legal justice. But often enough, in my experience, this kind of "advocacy" is all about convincing jurors or a judge about a perceived wrong that must be righted by financial recompense. It's all about money, especially for the lawyer.

This is not the kind of advocacy in today's gospel. When Jesus promises to send an advocate, the Spirit of truth, it really does concern the truth and really is someone who will stand with us in our trials. And we are not charged for this service.

The Greek word for Advocate (*paraklêtos*, "one called alongside," "helper") implies someone who comes to another's defense and provides that person the tools needed to speak the truth. Jesus speaks of this Advocate as one who "proceeds from the Father" and gives true testimony to Jesus. In fact, other passages lay out various aspects to this Advocate, but he is identified clearly as the Holy Spirit, the Spirit of truth. There is a direct and coherent line, then, between the Father and the Son and the Holy Spirit. All three are on our side. And once the Son returns to the Father, as Jesus did in his ascension, the Spirit is sent to be our advocate, our guide. This is the same Spirit we await at Pentecost, toward which the liturgies are now building.

Meditation: Take time to reflect on the nature of the Holy Spirit. The Paraclete, or Advocate, is a major image for the Spirit from John's gospel. What other images come to mind? How do you experience the Spirit in your own life?

Prayer: Praised be you, Lord God, heavenly Father, and praised be you, Lord God, only begotten Son! Send us the Spirit you have promised to accompany us as we proceed to spread the good news of your love for the world.

Believe!

Readings: Acts 16:22-34; John 16:5-11

Scripture:
"Believe in the Lord Jesus and you and your household will be saved." (Acts 16:31)

Reflection: Some years ago, the city of Baltimore, Maryland, chose as a motto "Believe!" It was plastered on billboards and painted on sidewalk benches and in parks. The city is a wonderful place to live but one filled with many urban problems and a lot of violence and poverty. The purpose of the motto was likely to instill some pride in the city's residents. Believe in yourselves. Believe in the city. Believe in your neighbors. Don't let the undeniable difficulties of everyday life get you down. There were some skeptics, of course, who mocked the motto. They wondered what we were supposed to "believe." But this verb is a powerful one, and it is front and center throughout the Easter season.

The marvelous story of the arrest of Paul and his companions in Philippi recounted in today's first reading illustrates the theme of belief. After their miraculous release from their chains but their refusal to escape the jail, the bewildered jailer asks them, "Sirs, what must I do to be saved?" That is exactly the question the apostles were waiting for. They have just the answer: Believe in the Lord Jesus.

For followers of Christ, believing is not some vague expression. There is no mystery about the *object* of belief. It is a person. We believe in Jesus Christ and no other. He is the reason we celebrate this entire season of Easter. Moreover, we wish to share him with others, for all are invited to partake in the salvation he has achieved through his death and resurrection.

Baltimore went on to seek out new mottos once the old one had faded. But there is no moving on beyond Jesus Christ. He is the fulcrum of our faith, the center of our universe.

Meditation: Reflect on the quality of your belief in the Lord Jesus. How is he at the center of your own faith, indeed, your own existence? Can you identify other aspects of "belief" that are operative in your life?

Prayer: Lord Jesus, I confess you as my Lord and Savior and I honor you for blessing me in multiple ways. Give me the grace to stay focused on you and to be willing to share you with others.

A House Divided

Readings: Acts 17:15, 22–18:1; John 16:12-15

Scripture:
When they heard about resurrection of the dead, some began to scoff, but others said, "We would like to hear you on this some other time." (Acts 17:32)

Reflection: Although not a formal member of a Christian denomination, Abraham Lincoln read the Bible assiduously and used it in many of his talks. Famously in 1858, when slavery was a hot topic, Lincoln gave a campaign speech that became known as the "house divided" speech because it used a biblical image (Mark 3:25; Matt 12:25) to show why the United States could not afford to have two types of states, slave states and free states. As in Jesus' teaching, he felt that a divided house could not long survive. Thus he pushed hard for preserving the Union.

One of the elements that apparently divided some of the early Christians was the very notion of the resurrection. Today's first reading indicates that Paul's preaching on the resurrection received mixed reviews. But elsewhere, the gospels show that it was not a concept that engendered a lot of unity (1 Cor 15:12). To this day, even some Christians try to water down the concept of the bodily resurrection of Jesus and the promise that we will be raised from the dead as well.

Some see it as simply a notion that the "spirit" of Jesus lived on in his followers. Others view it as ongoing life through the endless chain of disciples who continue to proclaim the gospel message.

Despite the controversy over resurrection, the Easter season is the affirmation that it is absolutely, uncompromisingly central to Christian faith. The appearance stories of the risen Jesus defy logical explanation. Nothing, however, can fully explain how a small group of frightened apostles, huddled behind locked doors in the city where their Master was humiliatingly crucified, could be transformed into the bold evangelizers they became. Their faith was neither in an empty tomb nor a vague recollection of what Jesus had taught. It was rooted in an experience of Jesus Christ alive and leading them onward. Only the resurrection can explain this dramatic about-face.

Meditation: How would you explain the transformation of the early apostles into bold heralds of the gospel? Do you believe that Christianity could exist without the resurrection? Open up a discussion with some of your family, friends, or church members. What do they think of the resurrection?

Prayer: Lord God of heaven and earth, lead me more deeply into the mystery of the resurrection of your Son, through the gift of your Spirit, so that I might proudly proclaim my faith with confidence.

Just a Little While

Readings: Acts 18:1-8; John 16:16-20

Scripture:
"A little while and you will no longer see me, and again a little while later you will see me." (John 16:16)

Reflection: Years ago, when I was first learning Spanish, I lived for several months with a hospitable family in a small town in Mexico. I quickly learned that many Mexicans used the expression *"ahorita vengo"* ("I'll be back in a little while") with a very loose time frame. The wife in my household used it unceasingly. It could mean anything from five minutes to five hours or more! That made a big difference to me when I was wondering what time the next meal was going to be served.

Jesus' saying in today's gospel perhaps is similarly indistinct. Christians have been awaiting his return in glory—something to which the other gospels allude (Matt 23:30; Mark 13:32-33)—for some two thousand years. Just how long is "a little while"?

Acts is a book that reflects the church's realization that God's time frame is not our own. Since it tells the story of the church's extended life after the resurrection and the coming of the Holy Spirit, it shows that Christians had finally adapted to this uncertain calendar while not losing sight of sustained hope in that promised second coming.

When my stomach was growling in Mexico, I anxiously hoped that the "little while" would indeed be a short time. But patience wears thin under duress. The question for us today is how to sustain our patience while we anticipate what Jesus always promised.

Meditation: If you feel sometimes as confused about Jesus' promise of a "little while," you are not alone. If we are honest with ourselves, we often are impatient for God to act and act now. Take time to take your own pulse with regard to patience. How well are you sustaining it? Will it endure?

Prayer: Lord, I look forward to your promises and await their fulfillment with hope. Grant me patience so that I may not waiver in my faith. I promise to do my best, and with your grace, I will persevere.

May 13 (Thursday) or May 16: The Ascension of the Lord

Starstruck

Readings: Acts 1:1-11; Eph 1:17-23 or Eph 4:1-13 (longer form) or 4:1-7, 11-13 (shorter form); Mark 16:15-20

Scripture:
"Men of Galilee, why are you standing there looking at the sky?" (Acts 1:11)

Reflection: Most people are drawn to unexpected and unusual events. They attract our attention precisely because they are out of the ordinary. Not long ago, I was on my way with a friend to a restaurant where we had made a reservation, because it was popular and hard to book. The evening was warm, and the residential neighborhood quaint. We had parked the car and were about to walk to the restaurant when, all of a sudden, I caught sight of, and heard, a small group of people with instruments a few blocks away, coming our way. They appeared out of nowhere playing intriguing music with strange instruments, dancing up the street. It was just an ordinary summer's evening. We stood enraptured, for the scene was at the same time charming and mesmerizing. What a motley band! But their music was very tuneful; we found ourselves tapping our feet to the rhythm. To this day, I have no idea why they were there; they just disappeared up the street. But we nearly missed our reservation!

I can empathize with the disciples at the ascension. Looking up at the sky, indeed! Their Master was taking his leave in a most unusual way. They were naturally drawn to the extraordinary event. Intriguing it must have been. Entrancing perhaps. But the angel's question draws them back to earth. What are you doing gazing heavenward? Are you starstruck? Your task is down here. Don't you remember? You are supposed to get moving, to ignite the fire of evangelization. Come back down to earth!

Meditation: The ascension is an extraordinary moment of leave-taking. It may have been the event the disciples dreaded, when they would be left alone with the mission. But not alone really, for Jesus' going meant the coming of the Spirit. What would your feelings have been in such a situation? How do you view our task on earth now?

Prayer: Lord, help me focus on what my task here on earth is. You have gone to the Father to prepare a place for us, but you have charged us to fill your shoes. Help me do this effectively.

May 14: Saint Matthias, Apostle

Who Chooses Whom?

Readings: Acts 1:15-17, 20-26; John 15:9-17

Scripture:
"It was not you who chose me, but I who chose you and appointed you to go and bear fruit that will remain." (John 15:16)

Reflection: The tale has been told in various ways in movies as well as in real life. A group of boys is organizing some sports by divvying up into teams. The really athletic types do the choosing. Inevitably, one or more of the available participants—with little ability in sports but often a strong desire to do well—don't get chosen until the very end. Or they are chosen with great reluctance, perhaps for fear they will do more harm to the team than good. Anyone who has experienced this situation knows how it feels to be left out. Sometimes, of course, especially in the Hollywood scenario, the underdog ends up an unexpected hero. Life does not always imitate art in this regard.

The choice of Matthias in today's first reading says more about the symbolic importance of the Twelve than it does about Matthias himself. Like most of the Twelve, after the choice is made by lots, he disappears into the mists of early Christian history. Yet he was chosen. He did not volunteer, nor did he choose. He was chosen, just as Jesus reminds the disciples in today's gospel that this is the way "vocation" works. Sometimes we may think we are the ones who have made the choice, but God's grace works discreetly behind the scenes to give lie to this illusion. God chooses us, unworthy vehicles though we may be, to do his will.

On this feast day, in particular, it is good to recall the functioning of the Twelve as that chosen inner circle who were intended to guarantee the apostolic foundations of the church. While one of the original Twelve (Judas Iscariot) proved himself totally unworthy by his act of betrayal, the choice of Matthias kept the group as a whole intact to fulfill Jesus' vision of a new people.

Meditation: Reflect on your own "vocation." When did you come to realize what your true vocation in life was? Do you feel called, chosen by God for any particular task?

Prayer: Almighty and ever-living God, thank you for the gift of my vocation. You knew me before I knew myself, and you called me out of love. For this great mystery I rejoice and give you thanks.

May 15: Saturday of the Sixth Week of Easter
(USA: Saint Isidore)

Ask and You Will Receive

Readings: Acts 18:23-28; John 16:23b-28

Scripture:
"Until now you have not asked anything in my name; ask and you will receive, so that your joy may be complete." (John 16:24)

Reflection: Is it too much to expect that Jesus wants us to be happy? Jesus says in today's gospel, "[A]sk and you will receive, so that your joy may be complete." The Lord wishes us to be joy-filled. Faith is not expected to make us sad or to burden us. It is supposed to lead to joy.

I fear many Christians—and Catholics are no exception—have a conception of faith as something that inevitably burdens us and hardly leads to true joy. Yet that is the opposite of faith. Note that Jesus also reminds his disciples that they had not yet asked anything "in my name." The Father is one who responds to requests honestly made in Jesus' name. Were the disciples too timid to ask? Did they fear offending the Lord by asking for too much? Too little?

A smile came to my face when I realized that today is also the optional memorial of St. Isidore. He was a Spanish farm worker from the eleventh century, reputed to care for the poor and needy. I don't know much about this farmer, but I wonder if he boldly asked God for blessings on his crops. Something must have worked, for he became the patron saint of farmers.

This gospel passage is not the only one where Jesus encourages his followers to ask in order to receive. In the Sermon on the Mount, Jesus says essentially the same thing. "[A]sk and it will be given to you; seek and you will find; knock and the door will be opened to you" (Matt 7:7). Sometimes people complain that they have petitioned God in prayer for one favor or another and not received it. This has made them doubt their faith. But the issue is not whether we received exactly what we wanted but rather what might be good for us. Joy is a deep, interior feeling and not something rooted in accumulating more things or responding to our whims. To ask with faith is to ask boldly in Jesus' name but also to pray, "your will be done" (Matt 6:10).

Meditation: Have you learned to be bold in your prayer? Do you ask freely, seek with conviction, knock so that the door will be opened? Examine the quality of your prayer life, and resolve to pray more regularly, more intently, and with more faith, so that you can also pray but "your will be done."

Prayer: My Father in heaven, be gracious to me and give me all that I need to lead a good and faithful life. May your will be done on earth as in heaven!

May 16: Seventh Sunday of Easter

The Deeper Unity

Readings: Acts 1:15-17, 20a, 20c-26; 1 John 4:11-16; John 17:11b-19

Scripture:
"Holy Father, keep them in your name that you have given me, so that they may be one just as we are one." (John 17:11b)

Reflection: We pray for it regularly. We tout that it is our goal. In January, we celebrate a week of intense prayer for it every year. Yet one of the most scandalous aspects of Christian faith remains: the divisions in the Christian community that mar the *unity* of the Body of Christ.

I remember being taught, as a boy in Catholic grade school in a largely Protestant town, to avoid ever entering a Protestant church, several of which I had to walk past on my way to and from school. What went on in there that was so dangerous? I grew up with Protestant friends in the neighborhood. Yes, we recognized that we came from different traditions, but I did not perceive that we were, deep down, terribly different. Of course, I had a lot to learn as I matured. But by then, the Second Vatican Council (1962–65) had begun and a phenomenon called "ecumenism" had taken off. Many Catholics had high hopes that we could begin to repair the divisions in the church, the Body of Christ. Much progress was made, but over time, enthusiasm waned, the fires burned low, other priorities dominated church life, and divisions stubbornly remain.

In the midst of this situation, we recall on this Sunday in the Easter season that Jesus never expected or wanted divisions among his followers. It is our folly that has created these fissures. Sometimes differences are over serious theological issues. Many times they are over much less serious issues of governance, authority, or customs that have built up over centuries. Jesus' great prayer in John 17, rightly called the high priestly prayer, is a fervent prayer that the deeper unity that exists between the Father and the Son would find fruit among his followers. He earnestly desired and prayed that we would be *one*. This cannot be a prayer for only the annual ecumenical week from January 18 to 25, as good a practice as this might be. It should be a daily prayer. Each of us should pray from the depths of his or her heart that the divisions that have accrued over the centuries may dissipate and that all Christ's followers will be one.

Meditation: How have Christian divisions marked your own life? Do you think they can be overcome one day? What steps can you take in your own life to promote unity among Christians?

Prayer: Lord, we do seek the unity to which we are called, but we are often too weak to bring it about. Come to our aid, show us the way, touch our hearts, and reconcile us to one another.

Plain Talk

Readings: Acts 19:1-8; John 16:29-33

Scripture:
"Now you are talking plainly, and not in any figure of speech." (John 16:29)

Reflection: In my ministry as superior general of an international community of diocesan priests, I had to visit many different countries in five continents. As expected, I encountered many different customs in these countries. Even simple things, like communicating clearly in plain language could be complicated. On one occasion, I had to meet with an African bishop who was very refined, kind, and welcoming. What I did not know was that the custom in his culture was basically to speak in roundabout language about delicate matters. There I was, an American with a tendency to "tell it like it is" and not "beat around the bush." I was used to plain talk. In the course of the conversation, this bishop would tell stories, but I was getting frustrated at wanting to bring the conversation to closure. We needed to reach an accord, but we seemed to be going in circles. In reality, I had to learn that all his stories made some point related to what we were discussing. But I sure wished I had had an American conversation partner.

I can thus identify with the disciples' frank admission: "Now you are talking plainly." It must have been frustrating for the disciples in John's gospel to hear Jesus speak in vague, symbolic, figurative language. Cut to the chase! What do we need to do to understand what you mean by "a little while"? How should we follow you, Jesus?

Throughout this Fourth Gospel, Jesus regularly speaks in roundabout and symbolic ways. The vocabulary is often simple—concepts like light, darkness, bread, sheep, and shepherd—yet they hide far deeper meanings. To understand his words requires that we sit with them, let them sink in, and mull them over. As I eventually was able to do with the African bishop, we need to find ways not to object to Jesus' mysterious message but to engage it for what it is: an invitation to life.

Meditation: What parts of John's gospel that we have been hearing throughout the Easter season are most elusive for you? Take time to identify one or two images from the Gospel and sit with them for awhile. Don't be afraid to ask the Spirit to come and help you interpret the message.

Prayer: Loving and merciful God, forgive me if I have sometimes been impatient with your Word. I am open to learning how to plumb the depths of your message for me and for our world. Be patient, Lord, and I will get it.

Compelled by the Spirit

Readings: Acts 20:17-27; John 17:1-11a

Scripture:
"But now, compelled by the Spirit, I am going to Jerusalem."
(Acts 20:22)

Reflection: Our journey toward Pentecost advances. It dove-tails to a degree with Paul's own missionary journey. In the first reading today, Paul gives his farewell address to the presbyters of the church in Ephesus. In it he summarizes aspects of his missionary efforts, his humble service to the Lord, and his dual outreach to both Jew and Gentile. But there is a hint of foreboding in this farewell. Although he admits that he does not know what he will face as he heads to Jerusalem, he is "compelled by the Spirit" to continue on this journey in which he has faced innumerable trials and tribulations. He acknowledges that he likely will not see his audience again. So he is conscious of possible impending doom.

The compulsion of the Holy Spirit should give us some pause today. It is likely related to Paul's outburst to the Corinthians when he says, "If I preach the gospel, this is no reason for me to boast, for an obligation has been imposed on me, and woe to me if I do not preach it!" (1 Cor 9:16). Such compulsion Paul felt. It was as if nothing could stop him from proclaiming the truth of the gospel.

The compulsion of which we are speaking here is obviously not about obsessive-compulsiveness. Paul is still in control of his life. But he freely made himself available to the work of the Spirit so that he could fulfill the vision that was given to him at his conversion/call, namely, that he would give witness to the gospel by his sufferings. Many heroes of our faith that we admire are those individuals who felt this same compulsion. They had the irresistible urge to proclaim the truth, whether it was accepted or not. When Paul was not well treated in one place or another, he would move on, much as the Lord Jesus himself had done and had commanded his own disciples to do (for example, Matt 10:14). This is the kind of divine compulsion that helped the gospel to flourish.

Meditation: Have you ever felt any compulsion to put your faith in action? Perhaps when you prepared for your confirmation, you felt "on fire" and full of zeal. Perhaps that waned with time and life's inevitable obligations. How can you recharge your spiritual batteries to embrace your baptismal identity? Ask God's grace to do so.

Prayer: Lord, I do not always feel "compelled" to do what I should do to be faithful to my baptismal call. Give me courage to accept what I must do and the wisdom to know when I must simply move on.

May 19: Wednesday of the Seventh Week of Easter

Consecrated in Truth

Readings: Acts 20:28-38; John 17:11b-19

Scripture:
"They do not belong to the world any more than I belong to the world. Consecrate them in the truth. Your word is truth."
(John 17:16-17)

Reflection: There is no denying that we live in a world where "truth" has become a scarce commodity. Part of this is likely due to social media where, because of seeming anonymity and an impersonal venue, people can say almost any outrageous thing with impunity. Part of it is also a product of increasing divisiveness in the world. Most of us are sucked into the dualism of insiders and outsiders, winners and losers, the powerful and the weak. This environment has fostered a tendency to deny objective truth in favor of creating one's own version of it. Alternative "facts" become a new way of viewing reality, skewed though it might be. I can almost hear Pontius Pilate's searching question to Jesus: "Truth, what is that?" (John 18:38, my translation).

In today's gospel Jesus explains that his disciples do not belong to *this* world any more than he did. That is why they can also expect to suffer for the sake of being his followers. But Jesus also asks his heavenly Father to "[c]onsecrate them in the truth" and then defines truth as "[y]our word." To be consecrated in the truth must mean somehow to be so intimately tied to it that we cannot do otherwise than speak the truth. We cannot deceive or be deceived. We cannot lie. We have to remain faithful to the truth as we come to know it, under the guidance of the Holy Spirit. This means, in part, that it is to be found in God's own word, not our own. While it is true that the Scriptures can be bent to mean whatever we want them to mean, it is possible to read the Scriptures objectively, to hear them as truth, if we would but rely on the Spirit to guide our interpretations. If we, as Christians, cannot live more objectively in the truth than the general public, then I fear we are lost as a people. We must commit to the truth *in* this world and not simply await the truth in the world to come.

Meditation: What do you think it means to be "in the world" but not *of* it? How can we as Christians still live in a context of diversity and pluralism and still believe in objective, external truth? How are Jesus and his message related to truth?

Prayer: Consecrate me in your truth, Lord, as you promised to do for your followers. Enlighten my path so that I will know the truth when I encounter it and will defend and proclaim it with all my being.

Take Courage

Readings: Acts 22:30; 23:6-11; John 17:20-26

Scripture:
"Take courage. For just as you have borne witness to my cause in Jerusalem, so you must also bear witness in Rome." (Acts 23:11)

Reflection: One of the beloved films of all time appears periodically around Easter—*The Wizard of Oz* (1939). Besides being splendid cinematography with a great cast, it also offers a tale with some substance. Designed for kids but tailored to adults, we might say. One of the delightful characters is the Cowardly Lion. He is the one who lacks "courage" and is so anxious to find some that he willingly accompanies Dorothy Gale—the lost young heroine—on the mystical journey to the Wizard of Oz, who supposedly can provide all the features the characters lack. Alas, they eventually discover the Wizard is a fraud ("a good man but a bad wizard"). They are forced to look within themselves and to help one another to find what they need.

In my reading of Paul, both his letters and his story as told by Acts, I do not see a man visibly lacking in courage. He comes across as bold, sometimes even brash, and rather forceful. Yet there are hints in his story, already beginning with his conversion, that he will need all the courage he can muster, for he will suffer for the sake of Jesus.

Today's first reading tells of Paul before the Sanhedrin, shrewdly causing a division to occur during his defense. He cheekily recalls his Pharisaic background to claim he is being persecuted by the Sadducees for believing in the resurrection. (Pharisees believed in a general resurrection of the dead, whereas Sadducees did not.) That gets Paul off the hook then and there. But in a vision, the Lord says there is more in store. Paul will have to "bear witness in Rome." The Greek expression is the root for the English word *martyr*. Bearing witness ultimately can mean giving up your life. Ancient Christian tradition asserts that Paul was martyred in Rome, probably under Emperor Nero.

Meditation: Most of us will never be called upon literally to be martyred, though there are sufficient modern martyrs for the faith to give one pause. How can you best bear witness to the truth of the gospel? Could it involve defending life from natural conception to natural death? Opposing bigotry and anti-Semitism? Counteracting gossip and lies?

Prayer: Grant me courage, O Lord, to do whatever is necessary to bear authentic testimony to your will. Make up in my resolve whatever I might lack concretely as a courageous individual.

Rehabilitation

Readings: Acts 25:13b-21; John 21:15-19

Scripture:
"Simon, son of John, do you love me?" (John 21:17)

Reflection: The poignant scene between the risen Jesus and Simon Peter is worthy of serious meditation. Some scholars believe the story is a kind of "rehabilitation" of the chief spokesman of the Twelve apostles whose other claim to fame is having denied he knew Jesus, not once but three times (John 18:15-27 and parallels). Making the confrontation even more intriguing is that the original Greek words for "love" are not the same. The first time Jesus asks if Simon Peter loves him, the word he uses is the kind of deep, intense love one would need to lay down one's life for a friend (Greek *agapaō*). Peter quickly responds in the affirmative, but using a different word that describes the casual love one has for friends (Greek *phileō*). The second time, Jesus again uses the deeper word, pressing the point further. Peter's response repeats only the lesser word. The third time, Jesus seemingly accepts Peter's lack of depth but insistence that his love is genuine, for he uses the same word Peter does: Do you love (*phileō*) me as a friend? Peter is hurt by the third question but strongly insists that he loves (*phileō*) Jesus. Despite Simon's threefold affirmation that he does indeed *love* Jesus, it is not (yet) the deepest kind of love (*agapē*) to which the Christian community as a whole is called.

This interpretation is uncertain but quite possible. More important is that Simon Peter affirms his love for Jesus, for which he is given an important charge: shepherd my flock! In essence, the story confirms that this rehabilitation worked. Peter goes on to be the chief spokesman for the church, identified with the founding of the church in Rome and considered the first pope, the first in the line of apostolic Petrine ministry down to our own day. According to ancient Christian tradition, he too was martyred in Rome around the time of the Emperor Nero. Acts, in a sense, comes full circle. Peter had dominated the first third of the book and Paul the remaining two thirds. Both bore witness effectively, and literally, for the Lord.

Meditation: Pope Francis is the successor of Peter in our day and is our Holy Father. Take time today to pray for him and his successors. Call him to mind and ask the Lord not only to protect and guide him, but to give him the strength he needs to make the difficult decisions that belong to his office.

Prayer: Merciful Father, bless our Holy Father Pope Francis and all the bishops who collaborate with him in the college of bishops. May we never lack for authentic shepherds who will protect and lead the flock.

Boundless Testimony

Readings: Acts 28:16-20, 30-31; John 21:20-25

Scripture:
"Lord, what about him?" (John 21:21)

Reflection: As we near the end of the Easter season and the great solemnity of Pentecost, we focus once more on the importance of bearing witness to the faith. The entire season has been one long meditation on how Christian faith, rooted in the resurrection, was from the very beginning evangelical. Like the gift of love, it cannot be kept to ourselves. It must be shared. It is a story of boundless testimony that goes on and on, and in which we play our own small part.

One limitation to this scenario, however, is that we Christians sometimes are more concerned about others' roles in the drama of faith than our own. After the moving encounter between the risen Jesus and Simon Peter that we reflected on yesterday, Peter's words show that he has not quite gotten the focus right. "Lord, what about him?" Peter has not yet overcome the human tendency to wonder about the duties or fate of others. When he asks Jesus about the fate of the Beloved Disciple (never named in John!), the response is basically, "mind your own business and follow me."

There is a paradox in the Christian faith that should be recalled here. On the one hand, we are each individually loved for who we are. Think of Paul's great admission that Christ "has loved me and given himself up for me" (Gal 2:20) and the affirmation that God already formed us in the womb and called us each by name (Ps 139:13; Isa 43:1). On the other hand, we have also been called together. This is the testimony of Acts. It is also the great Catholic emphasis that we have been celebrating throughout the Easter season. Christ died not only for me individually, but for *us*, a family of faith. As Paul affirms: "[Y]ou [plural] are Christ's body, and individually parts of it" (1 Cor 12:27).

Meditation: Think of your life as surrounded by a series of concentric circles. Who is the innermost circle (probably family)? The next circle (perhaps close friends)? And the next (perhaps acquaintances, coworkers, fellow parishioners)? And so on. How do these various circles interrelate? How do they shape you, and what do you contribute to them?

Prayer: Gracious and loving Lord, how marvelous it is to dwell on the grand design that you have set for us human beings, the epitome of your creation! Make me conscious of the personal gift you have bestowed upon me, and teach me how I can participate more fully with your chosen family.

Hearts on Fire

Readings: Acts 2:1-11; 1 Cor 12:3b-7, 12-13 or Gal 5:16-25;
John 20:19-23 or John 15:26-27; 16:12-15

Scripture:
Then there appeared to them tongues as of fire, which parted
and came to rest on each one of them. (Acts 2:3)

Reflection: We arrive at the goal of our fifty days—the great
solemnity of Pentecost. The most common image associated
with this feast is fire. How appropriate it is! Yet we also know
that fire can be an ambiguous reality. I confess that I have
somewhat of a love-hate relationship with fire. As a young
boy, my parents taught my siblings and me the dangers of
"playing with fire," and sure enough I got burned a few
times when I did not pull my hand away quickly enough
from an open flame. But I was also fascinated by fireplaces.
A cold winter's evening was a wonderful time to sit in front
of a blazing fire—our house had a functioning one for a long
time—chatting, singing songs, or hearing our father tell tales
of his youth. (Someone recently sent me a fireplace app! A
nice look on the computer, and no fire danger!)

But I also experienced a house fire once, escaping out a
side door after foolishly opening the front door without
touching it and not realizing that's where the fire was. And
once I was trapped on a mountaintop for some hours when

an unexpected forest fire started on a hot, dry summer day in California. I felt a little embarrassed having to be escorted by firemen off the mountain through burning embers. These experiences pale when compared to the horrible 2019–20 fire season in Australia, where *firestorm* took on new meaning.

Yet fire is exactly the correct image for Pentecost. It is the day on which we celebrate God pouring fire into the hearts of the faithful disciples, gathered in fear in the Upper Room in Jerusalem. Without that divine spark, their fear could not possibly have been converted to boldness. They could have stayed locked up in their own little world cowering at the possible cost of discipleship and seeing it as a price too dear to pay. True evangelizers have their hearts on fire. They await no other impetus. They know the source of their strength and how to use it. So, let us rejoice this day. As the Easter season yields once more to Ordinary Time, may our very ordinary lives be filled with extraordinary courage to carry the Easter message forth to the ends of the earth.

Meditation: Have you ever been "on fire" because of some belief, some idea, some desire to change the world? Call to mind any experience of this you may have had and try to recapture it today. Pentecost provides one more chance to burn with the desire to live out your faith.

Prayer: Come, Holy Spirit, fill the hearts of your faithful, and enkindle in us the fire of your love. Strengthen us from this day forward to proclaim that "Jesus Christ is Lord, / to the glory of God the Father" (Phil 2:11). Alleluia!

References

April 14: Wednesday of the Second Week of Easter
Helen Prejean, *Dead Man Walking: An Eyewitness Account of the Death Penalty in the United States* (New York: Vintage Books, 1994).

April 16: Friday of the Second Week of Easter
Kenneth L. Woodward, "In Praise of Fragments," *Commonweal* 146, no. 15 (October 2019): 54–61.

April 20: Tuesday of the Third Week of Easter
Misericordiae Vultus, Bull of Indiction of the Extraordinary Jubilee of Mercy (April 11, 2015), 1.

April 27: Tuesday of the Fourth Week of Easter
Sermo 340, 1; PL 38:1483; my translation.

April 28: Wednesday of the Fourth Week of Easter
John Ruskin, *Modern Painters* (London: Smith, Elder and Co., 1856), 3:253.

May 7: Friday of the Fifth Week of Easter
Charles M. Schulz, *You're A Winner, Charlie Brown!* (New York: Fawcett Crest, 1960).

SEASONAL REFLECTIONS NOW AVAILABLE IN ENGLISH AND SPANISH

LENT/CUARESMA

Not By Bread Alone: Daily Reflections for Lent 2021
Mary DeTurris Poust

No sólo de pan: Reflexiones diarias para Cuaresma 2021
Mary DeTurris Poust; Translated by Luis Baudry-Simón

EASTER/PASCUA

Rejoice and Be Glad:
Daily Reflections for Easter to Pentecost 2021
Ronald D. Witherup, PSS

Alégrense y regocíjense:
Reflexiones diarias de Pascua a Pentécostes 2021
Ronald D. Witherup, PSS; Translated by Luis Baudry-Simón

ADVENT/ADVIENTO

Waiting in Joyful Hope:
Daily Reflections for Advent and Christmas 2021–2022
Catherine Upchurch

Esperando con alegre esperanza:
Reflexiones diarias para Adviento y Navidad 2021–2022
Catherine Upchurch; Translated by Luis Baudry-Simón

Standard, large-print, and eBook editions available. Call 800-858-5450 or visit www.litpress.org for more information and special bulk pricing discounts.

Ediciones estándar, de letra grande y de libro electrónico disponibles. Llame al 800-858-5450 o visite www.litpress.org para obtener más información y descuentos especiales de precios al por mayor.